CW00351063

HISTO
ANNAPOLIS
VALLEY

RURAL LIFE REMEMBERED

MIKE PARKER

NIMBUS
PUBLISHING

Acknowledgements

My thanks to Helen, Emily and Matt; Nimbus Publishing; Gary Castle; Patricia
Melanson, Canadian Agriculture Library, Agriculture and Agri-Food Canada; Garry
Shutlak and the staff of Nova Scotia Archives and Records Management; Carolyn
MacKinley and Helen Arenburg, Blair House Museum, Nova Scotia Fruit Growers'
Association; Bria Stokesbury, Kings County Museum; Brian Nelson, Greenwood Aviation
Museum; Kathy Alcorn and Fred Hutchinson, Association of Nova Scotia Land
Surveyors; Allie Craswell, Sara Keddy; Richard Skinner; Murray Saunders; Gordon and
Sylvia Palmer; Roger Ryan; Dave and Paulette Whitman; Chris Roop; Pat Hampsey;
Brian Tupper; Gordon and Helen Whalyon; Elke Huber; Barb Bishop; Kevin Wood;
Anne Perrier; Trudy Spinney; Doris Nichols; Sandra and Rod Coleman; Connie and
Dennis Veinotte; Tom Forrestall; Dr. Allan Marble; Jenny Morton; St. Clair Patterson;
Graham McBride; Barry Corkum; Charles Rawding.

Copyright © 2006 Mike Parker

All rights reserved. No part of this book may be reproduced, stored in a retrieval system or transmitted in
any form or by any means without the prior written permission from the publisher, or, in the case of pho-
tocopying or other reprographic copying, permission from Access Copyright, 1 Yonge Street, Suite 1900,
Toronto, Ontario M5E 1E5.

Nimbus Publishing Limited
PO Box 9166
Halifax, NS   B3K 5M8
(902) 455-4286

Printed and bound in Canada

Design: Terri Strickland

Library and Archives Canada Cataloguing in Publication

Parker, Mike, 1952-
Historic Annapolis Valley : rural life remembered / Mike Parker.

Includes bibliographical references and index.
ISBN 1-55109-583-1

1. Annapolis Valley (N.S.)—History. 2. Annapolis Valley (N.S.)—Rural
conditions. I. Title.

FC2345.A4P37 2006   971.6'33   C2006-905399-5

We acknowledge the financial support of the Government of Canada through the Book Publishing
Industry Development Program (BPIDP) and the Canada Council, and of the Province of Nova Scotia
through the Department of Tourism, Culture and Heritage for our publishing activities.

Contents

Preface

Canada is divided into seven geographic regions, each with unique physical and climatic features. The Atlantic provinces are included in the Appalachian region which covers much of eastern North America. Nova Scotia is dominated by the Atlantic Upland which stretches the length of the province from Yarmouth to Cape Breton Island, manifesting itself in five "fragments." These fragments are separated by lowlands scoured out eleven thousand years ago with the retreat of glacial ice. The largest of the fragments is the South Upland, which gradually rises from the Atlantic Ocean into a plateau that covers much of southern and central Nova Scotia. Its northern edge constitutes the South Mountain, which is comprised predominately of granite, slate, and quartzite. Much of the South Upland interior remains sparsely inhabited, largely because it is a desolate territory of countless bogs, swamps, eskers, boulders, hummocks, lakes, rivers, and streams. A second piece of the Atlantic Upland is the North Mountain, a two-hundred-dred-million-year-old volcanic basalt ridge with the Bay of Fundy to its back. Together, the two mountains follow a parallel course of 190 kilometres from Minas Basin in the east to St. Mary's Bay in the west. Nestled between them for much of that distance is the Annapolis Valley, or simply "the Valley," a commonly used colloquialism. Author and historian Harry Bruce writes, "The Annapolis Valley is a juicy gash in the old and stony crust of Nova Scotia… It is a corridor of fertility, an archetypical valley of lushness. Few valleys anywhere assert their physique as straight forwardly as this one."

The physical allure of the Valley is its diversity—seacoast and agricultural land, ocean basins and freshwater lakes, tidal rivers and mountain streams, marshlands and meadows, fishing ports and farming hamlets, urban towns and country villages. Historically, the Valley's heritage is as rich as its soil, with roots reaching back four hundred years. Through the lows and highs of war and peace, depression and prosperity, it has few equals in North America. From the earliest days of colonialism, the Valley was "one of the most embattled territories in the history of the New World" where the seeds of a future nation were planted, fought over, and cultivated.

There is an intrinsic sense of serenity one gets from the Valley that only those who live there, have lived there, or visited there can truly appreciate. Analogizing the words of Albert Bigelow Paine from 1908, it is a place to escape the fetters of "men who dig up and tear down and destroy, who set whistles to tooting and bells to jingling—who shriek themselves hoarse in the marketplace and make the world ugly and discordant, and life a short and fevered space in which the soul has a chance to become no more than a feeble and crumbled thing." Perhaps that explains in part why the Valley has, to this point, stemmed the wave of "rural exodus" that has seen some regions of Atlantic Canada experience population declines of ten percent or more. History shows that going down the road in search of employment is not a recent phenomenon. Valley people, like Nova Scotians in general, left in significant numbers a century ago but then it was to Boston, not Halifax or Alberta. While much of rural Nova Scotia reels under out-migration, studies indicate the Valley to be holding its own and in many respects thriving. This is a tribute to the "traditionalists" who steadfastly remain (or who have returned home), and to the "come-from-aways" who breathe new life into old.

Nova Scotians are passionate about their history. Nowhere is this more evident than in the Valley, where dedicated researchers and heritage groups, amateur and professional, have painstakingly documented in minute detail the history of every community of any size that ever existed. That being said, the sheer weight of documentation presents unique challenges and restraints on a single work such as this. The reader must bear in mind that *Historic Annapolis Valley* is first and foremost about a region, not individual communities, although many are included as part of the overall story. Being a photo essay, the book depends heavily upon images which have been selected with the intent of mixing time-worn subjects with new, less visible material to produce a more contemporary account. This book is but one interpretation which is meant to entertain, educate, and encourage further reading and study. The underlying theme throughout is people, mostly common people, because they have always been, and always will be, the Valley.

Map of Annapolis Valley

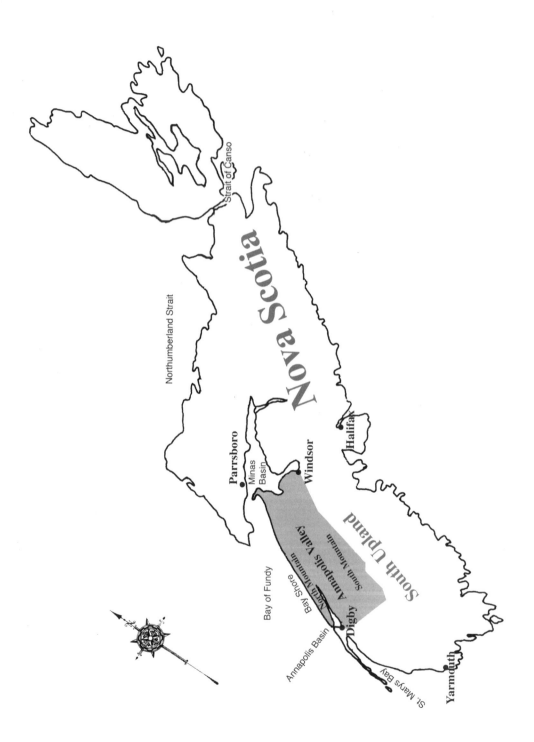

Strait of Canso

Northumberland Strait

Nova Scotia

Parrsboro

Minas Basin

Windsor

Halifax

South Upland

South Mountain

Annapolis Valley

North Mountain

Bay of Fundy

Bay Shore

Digby

Annapolis Basin

St. Marys Bay

Yarmouth

Chapter 1

Setting the Stage

ANNAPOLIS RIVER NEAR LAWRENCETOWN, 1920S

The Mi'kmaq knew the Annapolis River as *Teoopsig* meaning to "flow out between rocks," a reference to where the river passes through Digby Gut. The French initially called the river L'Équille for its abundance of eels then changed the name to Rivière Dauphin. When the British took permanent possession of Acadia in 1713, they renamed the river Annapolis to honour Queen Anne of England. Largest of the six Valley watersheds—the others being Gaspereau, Canard, Cornwallis, Habitant and Pereaux—the Annapolis River originates in the Caribou Bog between the town of Berwick and the village of Aylesford. Approximately one hundred kilometres long (estimates vary because of its circuitous route) the Annapolis is the only river of the six main systems that flows west into the Annapolis Basin, draining nearly two thousand square kilometres of land. Three other rivers, the Bear, the Moose, and Allain's, feed directly into the basin from their headwaters beyond the South Mountain. The Bear and Allain's formed part of two intricate canoe routes through the interior used by the Mi'kmaq for centuries to reach Nova Scotia's south shore.

DIGBY GUT, THE VALLEY'S WESTERN BOUNDARY

The tranquil beauty of the Annapolis Basin, accentuated by the North Mountain backdrop, is captured in an early 1900s panorama taken of berry pickers at Smith's Cove, Digby County. The picture provides a vivid portrayal of the ice age fissure the Mi'kmaq called *Toiten gisna Toitanog* meaning "gut" or "passage." Named St. George's Channel by the British, it was through this narrow mountain portal that the French sailed in 1605 en route to Port Royal. The Annapolis Basin, a sub-basin of the Bay of Fundy, is thirty-two kilometres in length from Digby to Annapolis Royal. French geographer Samuel de Champlain described it as "one of the most beautiful ports which I had seen on these coasts where two thousand vessels could be anchored in safety." The Loyalist town of Digby, founded in 1783, and for which the gut or gap is known today, marks the Valley's western boundary. Here, just inside Digby County, the mountains' parallel running course (east to west) continues sixty kilometres along St. Mary's Bay, the North Mountain forming a narrow finger known as Digby Neck which ends at Brier Island.

The eastern boundary of the Valley is less defined. Geologically speaking, it terminates at the mouth of the Gaspereau River near Wolfville, Kings County. By long-standing tradition however, and for the purposes of this book, the Valley extends eastward into Hants County approximately twenty kilometres to the town of Windsor. Both the Gaspereau and Avon Rivers, which flow into the Minas Basin, are a treasure trove for archaeologists and paleontologists. The Gaspereau has yielded Mi'kmaq stone artifacts thousands of years old, while on the Avon River at Blue Beach in 2005, the fossil of a prehistoric tetrapod dating back more than 350 million years was discovered, one of the oldest on record anywhere.

GASPEREAU RIVER (FOREGROUND) SHOWING COVERED BRIDGE AND OLD HIGHWAY 1, C.1950

The Gaspereau is the Valley's eastern "geological" boundary. The inconvenience of crossing the Avon River (visible in the distance) to conduct business was a primary reason for subdividing Kings County in 1781 to create the new county of Hants.

WINDSOR, C.1947

The town of Windsor, at the confluence of the Avon (foreground) and St. Croix Rivers, Hants County, is the Valley's "traditional" eastern boundary. Spanning the Avon River was critical to opening up the Valley to overland travel from the east. The first covered bridge in Nova Scotia was built in 1802 across the river narrows at Upper Falmouth. In 1836, the province's longest covered bridge (1150 feet) was completed where the highway and rail (foreground) bridges are shown in the photo. Construction began here in 1867 on a bridge for the Windsor and Annapolis Railway.

Pereau River, Nova Scotia

PEREAUX RIVER WITH MINAS BASIN IN BACKGROUND

Postcard view showing the mouth of Pereaux River, foreground, with Minas Basin and the eastern extent of North Mountain known as Blomidon in the far distance.

The Minas Basin, another sub-basin of the Bay of Fundy, was originally named Bassin des Mines by the French in the early 1600s for limestone and copper deposits discovered in the region. The four Valley rivers which empty into it—Pereaux, Habitant, Cornwallis, and Canard—all flow west to east, draining one thousand square kilometres of land. Cornwallis River is the longest, and like the Annapolis, originates in the Caribou Bog. The shortest is the Pereaux River at only four kilometres with a watershed of less than nine kilometres. Mi'kmaq legend says the Minas Basin was created when Glooscap, a native spirit deity, broke a beaver dam between Blomidon and Parrsboro allowing the Bay of Fundy to rush in.

The Valley is pie shaped, narrowing from approximately twenty kilometres in width at Minas Basin to five kilometres along the Annapolis Basin. It stretches 165 kilometres from Digby to Windsor, passing through all of Annapolis and Kings Counties, with a sliver of Digby and Hants Counties on the periphery. The North Mountain climbs sharply from the valley floor while the South Mountain appears to have a more subtle rise. Both reach heights of two hundred metres, which rates them little more than foothills when compared with classic mountain ranges.

Here at Minas Basin can be found some of the most enduring examples of Acadian dyke systems built to reclaim saltwater marshes for farming. Repaired, enlarged and maintained up to the present day, these marvels of early engineering design hold back the famed Bay of Fundy tides. With the richness of glacial soils and temperate climate, the Valley is one of the great agricultural regions of Canada, spoken of in the same breath as the Saint John River Valley, Niagara Peninsula, and Okanagan Valley.

CANNING AT LOW TIDE, C.1910

Postcard view of low tide at Canning on the Habitant River. In 1891 Canning boasted a population of 2,989, the largest in King's County; latest census reports put it at 811, fifth smallest among urban-encouraged "growth centres."

STEREOGRAPH OF PORT WILLIAMS

Stereograph of vessels high and dry at Port Williams on the Cornwallis River. A stereograph is a double-image taken of the same subject that when viewed through a stereoscope appears as one three-dimensional photograph. Developed in the 1830s and popularized by Queen Victoria in the 1850s, millions of such images were made until the late nineteenth century.

Twice daily the tides in Minas Basin rise and fall an average of twelve metres, the highest on earth, equating to thirty centimetres every twelve minutes, twenty-four hours a day. Heights can reach sixteen metres during a full moon causing a powerful tidal bore on some rivers. By comparison, the normal range between high and low tides for the North American east coast is between one and two metres. Sources claim the volume of tidal change in the Bay of Fundy, which amounts to one hundred cubic kilometres of water, equals the daily discharge from all the world's rivers. According to scientists well-versed in such matters, Nova Scotia actually bends when hit by the fourteen billion tons of sea water that flows into the Minas Basin.

**HABITATION,
PORT ROYAL**

This replica of the 1605 French settlement was erected in 1939 as a National Historic Site.

In 1603, Pierre du Gua Sieur deMonts was granted a French fur trade monopoly for all lands lying between the fortieth and forty-sixth parallels in northeast North America known as L'Acadie or Acadia—a term possibly originating from Mi'kmaq meaning "fertile land" or "territory." A year later, he spent a near disastrous first winter with his intrepid band of adventurers on ill-chosen St. Croix Island in the Bay of Fundy. Having explored the Annapolis River in 1604, deMonts and his scurvy-ravaged survivors sought refuge from their winter ordeal along the sheltered Annapolis Basin in the summer of 1605. It was there they erected a "Habitation" at Port Royal, establishing the oldest permanent European settlement north of Florida.

The Valley proved a major battleground for 150 years. In 1629, Scotsman Sir William Alexander, under English charter, built a fortified post (Charles Fort) six miles up river from the site of the French Habitation. The Habitation was burned to the ground in 1613 by Virginian privateer Samuel Argall. Three years after Charles Fort had been established, it reverted to France by treaty, was renamed Port Royal, and designated the capital of Acadia. War and peace would see the fort handed back and forth until 1710 when it was captured by the English for the last time. Thereafter called Fort Anne, the British defenders retained a tenuous hold for nearly forty years, repelling both French and Mi'kmaq attacks while remaining vigilant for enemy sails from the west. When colonial government moved to Chebucto with the founding of Halifax in 1749, Fort Anne remained an outpost for another century.

The British built Fort Edward in 1750 at Piziquid (Windsor) to guard against a rear attack on Halifax, maintain lines of communication, and disrupt French trade links along the Minas Basin with the French fortress of Louisbourg on Cape Breton Island. Like Fort Anne, it was garrisoned until the 1850s when all available imperial troops in Canada were withdrawn to fight the Crimean War.

Looking west from Fort Anne ramparts, Annapolis Royal   In 1917, Fort Anne was designated Canada's first National Historic Site.

Fort Edward Building, Windsor, N.S.

Fort Edward, Windsor   Only the blockhouse, oldest in Canada and a National Historic Site, remains today.

HAZELWOOD BROOK, BELLEISLE, C.1910

Acadia was a political pawn in distant European conflicts until 1713 when the Treaty of Utrecht ceded permanent possession to the British. Even then, however, the region remained in turmoil until the Treaty of Paris ended the Seven Years' War in 1763, when a calm settled over the Valley for the first time in one hundred years. At the epicentre of events for much of that period were the Acadians—French colonists named for the region they settled. By 1608, DeMonts and Champlain had turned their attention from Port Royal to the fur trade riches of Quebec. Following the loss of the Habitation in 1613 and dispersal of its settlers among the Mi'kmaq, little in the way of French colonization materialized until the early 1630s when approximately three hundred settlers—predominately tenant farmers from France—arrived in the Valley. Initially settling at LaHave along Nova Scotia's south shore, it became evident within a few years that while LaHave's fishery was prolific, its rocky, soil-depleted coast was not conducive to farming. The French subsequently packed up and relocated to Port Royal, which took in lands eastward along the Annapolis River as far as *Paradis Terrestre*—present-day Paradise. Melanson Settlement at Lower Granville near the Habitation dates its beginnings to 1667, and has been designated a National Historic Site owing to the fact it is the "only pre-expulsion Acadian settlement that has extended ruins with detailed historical documentation." Belleisle, between Annapolis Royal and Bridgetown, was populated by 1679, having as many as thirty Acadian homes around its marshes in 1755; archaeological digs have unearthed three foundations and thousands of artifacts here from the French period. The greatest expansion eastward in the 1680s reached the fertile lands of Minas Basin, which by 1755 was the most prosperous, populated Acadian district in the region with small settlements established at Grand Pré, Canard, Port Williams, Canning, Pereaux, Starr's Point, Wolfville, New Minas, Kentville, Gaspereau, and Windsor. Grand-Pré (meaning "large meadow") replaced Port Royal in the 1750s as the focal point for Acadian agriculture and commerce.

FARMING IN THE SHADOW OF NORTH MOUNTAIN'S BLOMIDON, 1950S

GRAND-PRÉ, HEARTLAND OF ACADIAN CULTURE AND HISTORY, LATE 1800S

**CLEARING LAND THE
ACADIAN WAY
USING MATTOCKS,
KENTVILLE, C.1912**

Considered lazy by contemporaries for not cutting down forests to make way for agriculture, the Acadians disproved their critics, being the first in North America to turn salt marshes into productive farmland. By doing so, they earned the nickname *défricheurs d'eau*—"clearers of water." Utilizing the most primitive of hand tools, Acadians constructed elaborate dyke systems, a technique long used in parts of France. An observer in 1710 wrote:

> The method was to plant 5 or 6 large trees in the places where the sea enters the marshes and between each row to lay down other trees lengthways on top of each other and fill the vacant places with mud so well beaten down that the tide could not pass through it. In the middle they adjusted a flood gate [aboiteau] in such a way as to allow the water from the marsh to flow out at low water without permitting the water from the sea to flow in at high tide.

Leaving marshes fallow for upwards of four years to allow time for snow and rain to wash away sea salt, Acadians reclaimed several thousand acres around Grand Pré and the Canard River. They also harvested coarse salt-marsh hay (spartina) which grew to the seaward of their dykes, laying it to dry on wooden platforms (staddles) built at a sufficient height to avoid rising tides. By doing so, the Acadians were able to feed their cattle throughout the year, a practice that differed from the norm which saw farm animals butchered in the autumn for lack of winter silage. This placed settlers in a vulnerable position come spring should replacement cattle not be readily available, a dilemma the resourceful Acadians avoided.

Predominately farmers, history has shown Acadians had salt water in their veins as they participated in the fishery and by the mid-1700s, operated ferry boats across the Minas Basin. They also carried on a lucrative export and import trade (some of it highly illegal) sending grain, cattle, and fur pelts to Louisbourg, Halifax, and New England in exchange for molasses, axes, clay pipes, gunpowder, rum, and fancy cloths.

HAYING NEAR WINDSOR, 1950S It would be the mid-1800s during the Agricultural Revolution before mechanical mowers and rakes such as this replaced the traditional sickle and scythe used for reaping.

STOOKING FLAX, C.1915 An Acadian crop staple, flax is still produced in the Valley today.

**FRENCH CROSS,
1890s**

When the Seven Years' War—last of the North American Wars—broke out in the colonies in 1754, it is estimated the Acadian population was between ten and fifteen thousand. Such numbers worried the British as they prepared to once again battle France for colonial supremacy, and despite repeated assurances of Acadian neutrality, Governor Charles Lawrence took it upon himself to act. In 1755, Acadians throughout the region had their lands confiscated and homes burned. Family ties were severed as thousands of Acadians were exiled to the New England colonies, Louisiana, and France. Some escaped, only to be apprehended and jailed in Halifax. Many were never caught while others died trying to escape. Repatriated in the 1760s, those who returned found their lands occupied by English-speaking colonists loyal to the British crown.

There have been few events in Canadian history so meticulously analyzed and criticized, commemorated and celebrated, as the Acadian deportation. Many testaments to *Le Grand Dérangement* are found throughout the Valley. Interest began in 1847, when Henry Wadsworth Longfellow's poem *Evangeline* was published in the United States. Today, the fictitious heroine's name graces a scenic trail, beach, school, and numerous businesses. Near Morden on the Bay of Fundy is the French Cross monument. Pictured above is one of four erected over the years—the first in 1756, the last, a stone cairn, in 1925; the cross featured was built in 1887 by John E. Orpin of Aylesford. This marks the approximate site where legend has it a number of Acadians fleeing Belleisle during the winter of 1755 died of starvation and were buried.

Most noted of the memorials is the Church of Saint-Charles at Grand Pré, built in 1922 by Acadians to honour the chapel where Colonel John Winslow established his headquarters to initiate deportation orders. Wolfville resident John Herbin, an Acadian descendant and historian, originally acquired the land in 1907 for preservation reasons. The Dominion Atlantic Railway purchased the property in 1917, erecting the Evangeline statue in 1920. The Canadian government assumed ownership of Grand Pré in 1957, designating it a National Historic Site in 1961.

Acadian culture and heritage are alive and well today with descendants numbering in the tens of thousands living throughout the Maritime provinces. Celebrations such as the Acadian Bicentenary at Grand Pré in 1955, and more recent events in 2004-2005 marking French colonization and the "Great Acadian Upheaval" have drawn international attention.

GRAND PRÉ CHAPEL, 1920s

ACADIAN BICENTENARY, GRAND PRÉ, 1955

SEEDING TIME IN KINGS COUNTY, C.1910

To plant the British standard, proclamations were issued in Boston during 1758 and 1759 inviting Protestants loyal to the Crown to take up residency upon vacated Acadian farms. Enticed with promises of generous land grants, freedom of religion and representative government, approximately eight thousand New England Planters (an Old World term for colonists) arrived in the Valley between 1760 and 1768. Predominately farmers, they came from Connecticut, Massachusetts, Rhode Island, and New Hampshire. Several townships of one hundred thousand acres were laid out in Annapolis and Kings Counties in the 1760s with every settler, by lottery, receiving equal portions of meadow, marsh, and timber lands. Arthur Eaton's *The History Of Kings County* tells us that settlement was initially restricted to the Minas Basin and the tidal limit of the Annapolis River—"that part of the Annapolis Valley…from Kentville to Paradise did not begin until some years after…because being beyond the flow of the tides it afforded no chance for village life." Valley settlement gradually spread with the arrival of Yorkshire farmers from England in 1772 and a trickle of New Englanders in 1775 with the outbreak of the American Revolutionary War. Following the defeat of British forces and evacuation of New York in 1783, the trickle became a torrent with thirty-five thousand United Empire Loyalists and disbanded soldiers descending upon Nova Scotia (which included New Brunswick until 1784), more than doubling its population. Unlike the Planters, who "brought with them all the goods and chattels necessary to re-establish their comfortable colonial lifestyle in the new lands," many Loyalists arrived as refugees with few possessions in hand. Some would leave, but the majority stayed, becoming the cornerstones upon which hundreds of Valley communities were founded. Eaton writes, "It is doubtful if any part of the wilderness of America of equal size was ever settled with people varying as much in race, religion, culture and social standing… English, American, Scotch, Irish, German and Dutch were intermixed by marriage or lived side by side, in every neighbourhood."

UNIDENTIFIED VALLEY FARM, 1930s

A stipulation of land grants in 1768 compelled settlers to plant two acres of hemp for making ship's rope. Hemp is being promoted today as a potential Valley cash crop.

BRIDGETOWN, 1890s

Bridgetown was one area of the Valley populated early by English settlers as it had been a crossing place since Acadian days for "hamlets" on the south side of the Annapolis River. Known originally as Hicks Ferry, the first bridge to span the river at this point was built in 1803, from which Bridgetown took its name in 1824. The covered bridge shown dates to the 1870s.

Historian Robin Wyllie credits the Planters with being "responsible for the foundation of much of Nova Scotia's nineteenth century industry." Every community had its industries and to provide more than a passing tribute is beyond the realm of possibility for a book of this nature. Physical traces of an earlier era have all but disappeared except for the occasional derelict building, crumbling stone foundation, or grassed-over mound indicative of something that once was. Much of it fell victim to fire (repeatedly in many cases) or simply died of old age with the changing times. Factorydale, Steam Mill Village, and Sheffield Mills bear testament to the importance industry played in the naming of those Kings County communities. W. A. Calnek in his *History of the County of Annapolis* provides a numerical listing of 368 "Industrial Establishments" for the year 1891. Not surprisingly, forty-eight were blacksmith shops which turned out an array of iron implements and tools needed to work the land, build ships, and keep horses, oxen, and conveyances moving. Some survived well into the twentieth century; Eugene Owens, an African Nova Scotian, operated this Bridgetown smithy until the 1960s.

An industry that made its mark but has received little attention is the manufacture of steel-edged tools (next page). Most noted of the earliest axe makers were Benjamin and George Eaton, Planter descendants from Lower Canard who crafted broad axes at Sheffield Mills and Berwick. Thomas Cox of Kentville (a first cousin of the Eatons) forged farm and wheelwright tools and was considered the best maker of single-bitted poll axes. There were also the Blenkhorns of Canning (James, Sydney, Hennigar, and Scott), descendants of Cumberland County Yorkshiremen who were noted shipwrights and axe makers extraordinaire. Through the years, the Blenkhorns survived three disastrous fires at Canning, one of which razed the town in 1866. The November 19, 1883, Halifax *Morning Chronicle* reported, "Blenkhorn & Sons, Canning, Kings County, ship 100 axes a day from their factory and employ fourteen hands." For decades, a double-bitted Blenkhorn axe was the tool of choice for choppers throughout the lumber woods of Atlantic Canada. Nothing remains today of the company except for its collectable axes and a few pictures such as these; after 120 years in operation Blenkhorn Axe Company finally succumbed to the power saw and closed out in the early 1960s.

BLENKHORN AXE COMPANY, CANNING

Sydney Blenkhorn, far left, was a second-generation axe maker who operated the business from 1890-1912.

BLENKHORN AXE COMPANY WHARF, CANNING, C.1912

Vessels carried hard and soft coal from Joggins and Parrsboro, Cumberland County, as well as from New York City and New Jersey, to fuel the forges.

GEORGE SWEET'S WHEELWRIGHT SHOP, LOCATION UNKNOWN, 1914

According to Barbara Roberston's book, *Sawpower: Making Lumber in the Sawmills of Nova Scotia*, there were 1,144 water-powered and steam-driven sawmills in Nova Scotia during the early 1870s, of which Annapolis County had seventy-five and Kings County sixty-three, ranking them sixth and eighth respectively out of eighteen counties. Wood was king with millions of board feet of lumber produced annually for export, shipbuilding, and various trades. Annapolis County had twenty-eight carriage-making factories alone in the early 1890s, fifth out of thirty-eight "industrial establishments" listed in Calnek's history. Perhaps the largest of that time was the Nova Scotia Carriage Company at Kentville, Kings County, which started operations in 1868. In the late 1890s, the business was manufacturing and selling more than three hundred carriages a year and employing thirty men; the 1907 catalogue listed thirty-four models of conveyance for sale. This would appear to have been the exception rather than the norm as Eaton writes in 1910 that "Kings County has had a few small manufacturing interests, but none of them have ever had great importance or have yielded their projectors much profit; the county is not a manufacturing county."

The years 1880 to 1910 were an especially busy period for companies entering the building supply and contracting business. The Valley is said to have been "well served" during that time, but if one company stands out, albeit briefly, it has to be Curry Bros. & Bent of Bridgetown. While many outlasted them, none from 1895 to 1899 came close to matching the company's output. Just for that reason alone they deserve special mention. Their story is twofold, beginning in 1858 with John Bath Reed who opened a furniture factory at Bridgetown. By 1880, he was turning out parlour furniture and bedroom suites, sofas, walnut chairs, and centre tables with marble tops. At the opposite end of the province in 1877, Rhodes Curry & Company of Amherst, Cumberland County, began producing a variety of building materials as well as school, office, church, and business furniture. Upon incorporation in 1891, the principal owners were Nelson A. Rhodes, Nathaniel Curry, and Mark Curry. Within two years, the company expanded into manufacturing railway and streetcars, which would eventually make them one of the province's most successful business firms with offices in Halifax, New Glasgow, and Sydney. In 1895, Mark Curry moved to Bridgetown to oversee an acquisition he, his brother, and Byron A. Bent had just made purchasing the J. B. Reed & Son furniture factory building at an "assignees sale." George Hutchinson, a graduate of the Boston Drawing School, was soon hired as foreman for the new firm, as was L. R. Fairn, the widely acclaimed architect whose work is seen throughout this book. For the next four years, Curry Bros. & Bent maintained a frantic construction pace. They built creameries in Windsor and Lawrencetown, the Royal Hotel in Wolfville, a train station in Wilmot and three others on the south shore, two railway engine houses at Yarmouth, a Baptist Church in Dalhousie, the *Berwick Register* newspaper office, apple warehouses in Port Williams and Berwick, an addition to Bloomfield school at Halifax, and a grandstand and other buildings for the Provincial Exhibition. Houses went up everywhere; in the summer of 1897, Curry Bros. & Bent built fourteen in the provincial capital. Then, for unexplained reasons described in the newspapers as the "latest development in the Curry Bros. & Bent difficulty," foreclosure took place in December 1899; the entire property was disposed of on February 7, 1900 at a mortgage sale. Of the sixty-eight contracts entered into between 1895 and 1899, records indicate that possibly only one, the new academy at Annapolis Royal, remained unfinished when the company shut down.

MAKING BASKETS AT PARADISE, EARLY 1900S

The Valley has been home to the Mi'kmaq for more than two thousand years although there is evidence Palaeo Indians, their ancient ancestors, first appeared at the end of the last ice age eleven thousand years ago. The Mi'kmaq or L'nuk ("The People") are part of the Eastern Wabanaki Confederacy of five Algonquin tribes, once the most populous and widespread of the North American First Nations. A semi-nomadic people, the Mi'kmaq wintered in the shelter of dense forests hunting and trapping, then summered along the coast to fish eels, salmon, and gaspereau, gather shellfish, and hunt porpoise and waterfowl. They called the first Europeans *nikmaq* meaning "my kin-friends" but history has shown drastic changes to their lifestyle ensued upon contact. First came the colonial wars, followed by settlers who cut down forests for lumber and agriculture, dammed rivers to drive the wheels of industry, and laid out town lots to accommodate their burgeoning numbers. Estimates vary as to how many Mi'kmaq originally lived in Nova Scotia, possibly fifty thousand or more, but due in large measure to introduced diseases such as small pox and tuberculosis, their numbers were reduced to approximately 1,700 by the late nineteenth century. Silas Rand (1810-1889), a Baptist minister from Cornwallis Township in King's County, became noted for his work with native people as an ethnologist, linguist, missionary, translator, and founder of the Mi'kmaq Missionary Society. Of the eleven languages he could read and write by the age of twenty-three, Rand preferred Mi'kmaq. He collected legends, translated scripture into Mi'kmaq, and compiled a Mi'kmaq dictionary of forty thousand words in 1849 that forms the basis of today's orthography. The majority of Nova Scotia Mi'kmaq in the 1800s lived in Annapolis and Digby Counties at scattered sites including Bear River, Lequille, Round Hill, Tupperville, Paradise, Lawrencetown, Brickton, and Middleton. The village of Bear River, among the first in Nova Scotia to have a native reserve (established in 1801), was widely known in the late nineteenth century for its Mi'kmaq fishing and hunting guides. Most native people, like twin sisters Agnes and Celia Labrador (above), eked out a meagre existence making traditional Mi'kmaq crafts such as sweet grass baskets, beadwork moccasins, porcupine quill embroidery, wood carvings, snowshoes, axe handles, and birchbark canoes.

MI'KMAQ FISHING GUIDE, NOEL LABRADOR, PARADISE

Four Mi'kmaq families—Luxie, Labrador, Phillip, Meuse—lived at Paradise in the early 1900s along the south bank of the Annapolis River on land known at different times as the "Public Lot," "Indian Lot," and "Glebe Land." There were a few small houses, supplemented by tents during the summer months, which would indicate permanent residency of some sort but sources claim Paradise was generally a seasonal campsite only. The Labrador family of two brothers and two sisters lived together in one of the houses. Stephen Labrador was described as "tall and stern" while younger brother Noel (above) was "bland, pleasant and very friendly." The women (Agnes and Celia) often worked in local homes doing domestic chores while the men guided American and local sportsmen fishing salmon on the river, for which they were paid five dollars a day. Another Labrador sister lived separately at Paradise with husband Peter Meuse who, in addition to being a river guide, was known for playing the violin and pump organ. Louis Jeremy, a Mi'kmaq from nearby Tupperville, was a skilled woodworker whose violins, baskets, bowls, ladles, cups, and saucers, carved miniature horses, carts, flowers, and boots are prized collectibles today.

The British garrison at Fort Anne called the Mi'kmaq "River People." It is understandable why two hundred years later Mi'kmaq Heggie Luxie considered the Annapolis River "My River."

Stephen Heggie Luxie, Sr., widely recognized as the last Mi'kmaq of Paradise, went by many names. In Mi'kmaq he was Ekien Laski. The French called him Étienne Alexis, the English called him Heggie Luzzie (or Luxie). Heggie was born on Christmas Day 1834 in Yarmouth County; his mother was Mi'kmaq, his father white. The family eventually moved to Port Lorne on the Bay of Fundy side of the North Mountain near Paradise. After living at Port Lorne for many years in a tent, Heggie struck out on his own, travelling extensively throughout Canada and New England. He and his wife Ellen (part Mi'kmaq, part French) had four children—son Steve and daughters Margaret (or Lena), Suse, and Rose. At some point, Heggie settled at Paradise but was banned from staying after he became involved in breaking up a domestic dispute which was seen as meddling by both the parties involved. Claiming to have the inherent right "to go on any man's land as long as the Queen [Victoria] lives," Heggie moved a short distance away and took up residency in the vicinity of the Leonard Road on railway property adjacent to a flooded gravel pit which came to be known as Heggie's Pond. In winter, the Luxies opened their cramped two-room home to youngsters skating and playing hockey on the pond so they could come in and be warmed by the fire. When Ellen passed away in 1900, Heggie stayed on at the gravel pit for another forty-one years.

**MI'KMAQ
PATRIARCH
HEGGIE LUXIE
(1833–1941)**

A life member of the Nova Scotia Guides' Association from its inception in 1909, Heggie's services as a river guide for salmon fishing were in great demand by both resident and American sportsmen; Heggie's son Steve and grandson Charlie also guided Americans at Paradise. When 102 years of age, despite failing eyesight and hearing, Heggie still walked without a cane, claiming his secret to longevity was rising every day at four o'clock in the morning to take a one-mile walk. Heggie Luxie died at the age of 108 in Soldiers' Memorial Hospital, Middleton, one month after his daughter Suse passed away. Most famous of the Annapolis River fishing guides, his obituary read in part, "none knew the pools or the art of fishing as well as he… He was patriarch of the Micmac [sic] Indians in Nova Scotia." The entire Luxie family is reportedly buried in the Roman Catholic Cemetery at Bridgetown but no grave markers can be found.

**FOUR UNIDENTIFIED
LADIES STROLL
ALONG RAILWAY
STATION PLATFORM
AT BRIDGETOWN,
c.1920**

Black history has four-hundred-year-old roots in the Valley dating to 1605 when Mathieu d'Acosta arrived at Port Royal as part of the French expedition, giving him the distinction of being the first individual of African descent in Canada. Eleven of the forty-eight Nova Scotia communities identified as having historical significance for Black heritage are located in the Valley. Historian Arthur Eaton writes that "in the 18th Century, slavery existed in almost all the chief Nova Scotia towns, the Kings County towns being no exception to the rule." He further describes how descendants "from slaves brought to the county by the early planters or purchased after they settled here" later formed settlements at Pine Woods and Gibson Woods near Kentville. In 1901, the Black population for Kings County was listed at 210.

The muster roll of 1784 Loyalists and disbanded troops for Annapolis County mentions 230 "servants" in and around Annapolis Royal. Historian W. A. Calnek writes in his county history of 1897 that Blacks "settled in considerable numbers in Digby, Clements and Granville but especially the former...where descendants are still to be found." At Annapolis Royal, the last slave was sold in 1804, although they were considered chattel and "willed" to surviving relatives for many years, possibly until slavery was abolished July 31, 1834. One of the more prominent, but seldom heard of Annapolis County communities, is Inglewood at Bridgetown. Settled in the 1850s by Loyalist descendants, a monument was erected there in 1977, commemorating Inglewood as the birthplace of the African United Baptist Association founded in 1854 by the highly acclaimed Black preacher, Reverend Richard Preston.

UNIDENTIFIED
COUPLE,
POSSIBLY COOKS
AT A YMCA CAMP
ON GOAT ISLAND
IN ANNAPOLIS
BASIN, C.1897

LUCY MITCHELL OF
GRANVILLE

It was common for slaves to assume the surnames of their former masters. Arthur Eaton lists the "chief" family names for Pine Woods in Kings County as Bear, Jones, Landsey, Smith, Bell, Higgins, Lawrence, and Powell. In many cases history has left us with given names only. Local historian Elizabeth Coward documented a number of male names in and around Bridgetown—Cato, Pompey, Primus, Jupiter, Caesar, Aesop, Plato, Sipio. Given names for Black women tended to be less flamboyant—Dinah, Nance, Clarinda, Patty, Letisha, and Venus.

Much has been written of Rose Fortune, a freed slave from Philadelphia, who lived at Annapolis Royal from 1783 until her death in 1864. Considered among the town's "most notable figures," she is hailed as one of Nova Scotia's "first Black entrepreneurs," a distinction earned for providing travellers with a wheelbarrow baggage pick-up and delivery service. Granville's Lucy Mitchell was also interesting but lesser known. Dubbed "Crazy Luce," not for a mental deficiency but in reference to her wild attire and penchant for tambourines, Lucy belonged to the Salvation Army, working as a domestic at a house west of Bridgetown. Known for her kindness toward children but possessing a volcanic temper, Lucy once chased an Englishman who had insulted her through the streets of Bridgetown, an incident caricatured by a local artist. Lucy died in 1910 at the age of one hundred.

HIGHWAY 101 EXIT SIGN

Every day, hundreds of motorists drive past Exit 8A for Ben Jackson Road along Highway 101. Few, if any, know the story behind the name. While William Hall is widely documented as the first Black and first Nova Scotian to win the Victoria Cross, Ben Jackson's own distinguished military career is often neglected, surprising considering how similar the two men's personal histories are. In fact, Hall and Jackson grew up within three miles of each other and knew each other well. Hall was born at Horton Bluff, Kings County, and Ben Jackson at Horton Mountain (now Lockhartville). Both went to sea at sixteen years of age—Hall in 1845, Jackson in 1851. Hall sailed first as a merchant seaman, then joined the U.S. Navy before switching to the Royal Navy. He earned the Victoria Cross in 1857 at the Relief of Lucknow during the Indian Mutiny. Jackson served aboard local square riggers the world over. In 1864, he was "pressed" into serving with the Union Navy during the American Civil War while on a stop-over in New York. Taking an assumed name, Louis Saunders, Ben's military career lasted just over a year, a hand wound leading to an honourable discharge and a war bonus of nine hundred dollars in 1865. During his stint, however, Ben served with distinction on several warships, and he was therefore entitled to a lifetime U. S. military pension of seventeen dollars per month (increased to twenty dollars at age seventy-five). After recovering

BEN JACKSON

from his injury at home, Ben went back to sea on
merchant ships until 1875, when he returned to Horton Mountain and for the
next thirty years farmed, peddled fish and vegetables, and collected his pension.

Hall, a life-long bachelor, came home to farm on Bluff Road near
Hantsport where he lived with two sisters until his death, August 25, 1904.
Ben Jackson, twice married and father of five children, was blind with cata-
racts when he passed away August 20, 1915. Both men's funerals drew large
crowds and both were buried without honours in unmarked graves at Stony
Hill Baptist Cemetery, Lockhartville. After much searching, William Hall's
body was located in 1945 and re-interred at Hantsport Baptist Church, a spot
more befitting a Victoria Cross winner. The location of Ben Jackson's grave,
unfortunately, remains unknown. Both men left their mark, however: one on
the pages of history, the other on the side of the road.

Chapter 2

Getting Around

SHADES OF TOM SAWYER

The three sportsmen in this early 1900s image opted for a Tom Sawyer-like conveyance to fish the backcountry of Digby County. Functional but short on design and freeboard for keeping feet dry, they would have been well advised in staying close to shore. In fact, the Mi'kmaq perfected the earliest mode of water transport, their birchbark canoe ideally suited for navigating Nova Scotia's interior labyrinth of lakes, rivers, and streams. The frail looking but solidly built craft also proved to be incredibly seaworthy. Paddling canoes upwards of eight metres in length equipped with sails, native people routinely crossed the Bay of Fundy to New Brunswick and more distant ocean waters to Newfoundland. The first Europeans were quick to recognize the canoe's merits and adopt its use.

BARQUE *KINGS COUNTY*, SUMMERVILLE, AVON RIVER, 1909

As Nova Scotia is a sea-bound province, early trade and travel were dependent upon shipbuilding. Along the rivers and basins of the Valley and Fundy shore, virtually every community with enough water to float a boat had a sawmill, shipyard, and builder of note. As early as 1740, sixteen Acadian vessels ranging in size from eight to thirty tons are said to have been trading with Louisbourg. John Parker writes in *Sails of the Maritimes* that in the late 1800s the Minas Basin turned out "a vast number of square-rigged ships, barques and smaller vessels." Of the thirty built by Ebenezar Cox at Kingsport between 1876 and 1890, the *Kings County* (above) was one of only two four-masted barques ever constructed in Canada. In 1909, it had the distinction of being the last square-rigged vessel to carry a cargo out of the Minas Basin.

Annapolis County historian W. A. Calnek wrote of the Bay of Fundy coast that "shipyards were to be found plentifully sprinkled along its shores, from which every year numbers of new vessels of all sizes were added to the mercantile marine of the Province." The Annapolis Basin and its tributaries also has a rich shipbuilding heritage. North America's first shipyard was established in 1606 by the French at Port Royal, where Pontgrave built two small vessels—a barque and shallop. Few today realize the extent of shipbuilding on the Annapolis River because it has been landlocked since the early 1960s after a causeway was built at Annapolis Royal. High tide once reached Paradise, thirty kilometres east of the old garrison town, where at least six builders turned out small vessels (circa 1815 to 1840), then floated them eight kilometres downriver to Bridgetown to have their masts stepped.

Bridgetown was a port of entry, where in 1823 alone, one hundred vessels were loaded with exports. L. D. Shafner built schooners at Bridgetown (from about 1888–1908) ranging in size from two hundred to four hundred tons. John Parker claims the *Peaceland*, 262 tons, built by Shafner for the Annapolis Shipping Company in 1919, was the last tern schooner to operate out of the Bay of Fundy and the last schooner built at Annapolis Royal.

KINGSPORT, 1940s

Kingsport on the Minas Basin, shown here in the 1940s, was once the busiest port in Kings County with coastal traders, ferries, and trains converging at its main wharf carrying freight and passengers.

BRIDGETOWN SHIPYARD AND WHARVES, ANNAPOLIS RIVER, C.1900

The first overland routes through the Valley were Mi'kmaq portage trails which generally followed water courses or crossed heights of land to avoid swamps and bogs. The Acadians incorporated these woodland footpaths into connector roads between their Port Royal and Minas settlements, remnants of which are still referenced as "Old French Roads." With the founding of Halifax in 1749, a stump-strewn road was immediately cut to Windsor, then later extended to Annapolis Royal to expedite the movement of British troops. The precursor of Highway 1 (making it the oldest road in Nova Scotia), the military road eventually evolved into the post road over which the Royal Mail was conveyed; large sections continue to be driven upon today. With the arrival of stagecoaches in the early 1800s, better roads were needed to meet the minimum speed requirement of eleven kilometres an hour. A series of "Great Roads" was built in the province, one being the Great West Road through the Valley from Halifax to Yarmouth. It would carry the first stagecoach between Halifax and Annapolis Royal in 1828, transporting both passengers and mail. Daily stages ran from Halifax to Windsor (the first in 1815), with seasonal tri-weekly service from Windsor to Annapolis Royal and weekly service between Annapolis Royal and Digby. Incorporating much of the post road into the new route, improvements were made in the "Great Road" by cutting the tops off steep hills, filling in hollows and changing course to include more level stretches. Statute labour maintained early roads, the daily pay being sixty cents and a gill of rum for ten hours work; extra rum but no money was offered as an incentive to work longer hours. The government initiated grants for settlers willing to establish stagecoach stops to provide shelter, food, and stables as fresh horses were needed every twenty-five kilometres. Secondary roads, or by-roads, were being cut out along the bases and over the summits of both North and South Mountains by the early 1800s, providing avenues for settlement and harvesting timber resources. In 1860, it was reported "the cross-roads and by-roads [were] too numerous to mention." Dempseys Corner, Ross Corner, and Keddys Corner are but three of many farming hamlets dotting the Valley countryside that owe their name to a settler, possibly the first, whose property bordered a crossroads.

EARLY POST ROAD, DIGBY COUNTY

Looking northeast along the post road where it crossed Highway 1 at Smith's Cove, Digby County. Parts of this old mail route are still driven upon today.

GREAT WEST ROAD NEAR SOUTH BERWICK, KINGS COUNTY

The Reformed Presbyterian Church began a colonial mission in the early 1820s, sending a wagon and preacher "to work among the settlers in New Brunswick and Nova Scotia."

The ways and means for settlers getting about were limited to walking or horseback until the early 1800s when wagons appeared in the Valley. Establishing a timeline is difficult but according to *The History of Kings County*:

> About 1803, it is said, Mr. Benjamin Belcher imported a wagon from Boston. The vehicle cost fifty pounds, and was an object of the greatest interest to the King's County people at large... It was not until 1823 that the first wagon was brought into Kentville. A tin peddler from New England came to the village with a white horse and a red wagon, bringing a load of tin-ware to sell. When he had disposed of his merchandise he sold his horse and wagon...and from miles around people came to see the remarkable 'turn out.' After that, two wheeled gigs and four-wheeled wagons gradually became common and horseback traveling steadily declined.

Numerous conveyances promoting everything from religion to milk to patent medicines and household utensils to apple seedlings, were common sights on late-nineteenth-century Valley roads. By 1902, Annapolis County had enacted eighteen regulations pertaining to peddlers or "hawkers" with three classes of license required. A pack license to walk about cost twenty-five dollars, a one-horse hawker's wagon license was seventy-five dollars, a two-horse, one hundred dollars. Failure to comply resulted in a fine and defaulting on immediate payment carried a maximum of thirty days jail time with hard labour.

Alfred C. Fuller (1885-1973) was perhaps the Valley's most famous "hawker." Born near Grand Pré, Fuller moved to Boston, as did many Nova Scotians, to find work, following in the footsteps of five brothers. From an initial outlay of fifty-five dollars for equipment and materials, the twenty-one-year-old entrepreneur began manufacturing wire brushes and selling them door-to-door in 1906 based upon a business plan designed by one of his brothers, who had recently passed away. Within four years of having an inventory of only five models to choose from, Fuller employed seven men in a factory, twenty-five agents in the field, and was doing forty thousand dollars a year in business. By 1921, Alfred C. Fuller owned 135 branch offices, had 2,400 salesmen knocking on doors, and was grossing $10 million annually. When he sold the company in 1943, a Fuller Brush representative was calling on nine out of every ten American homes, with annual sales of $30 million.

VALLEY "HAWKERS"

Vendors such as V. V. Aylward Dairy, Falmouth, went door-to-door through the Valley well into the 1900s selling produce, milk, meat, and fish. Alexander Robert Stirling of Greenwich, who by the mid-1900s was the largest apple grower in Canada, started out in the 1920s selling three hundred quarts of milk by horse and wagon to Wolfville residents.

VALLEY "HAWKERS"

The Rawleigh's Man, seen here at Annapolis Royal, represented an American company started in 1889 by W. T. Rawleigh "with only fifteen dollars, a borrowed horse, mortgaged buggy and four types of medicines." By the 1920s, the company produced and distributed more than one hundred household products and had twenty million customers in the United States and Canada.

A STEAM
LOCOMOTIVE
APPROACHES
BEAR RIVER
BRIDGE, 1956

The railway opened up a new era in trade and travel. For landlocked communities in the heart of the Valley it was a time of growth and prosperity. For traditional shipping ports serviced by the railway, life went on; for those beyond the tracks, it was a death knell.

The first passenger train from Halifax to Windsor entered the Valley in 1858 along the Nova Scotia Railway. The last pulled out of Kentville on the Dominion Atlantic Railway September 16, 1993. The intervening 135 years is a complex story of mergers, bankruptcies, boom and bust, private enterprise, and government intervention. In the beginning, railway construction was carried out on two fronts: from the east—Windsor to Annapolis Royal, 1869-1872—by the Windsor & Annapolis Railway Company, and from the west—Yarmouth to Digby, 1874-1879—by the Western Counties Railway. The first train from Halifax to Annapolis Royal ran in 1872; the first from Yarmouth to Digby in 1879. It would be 1891, however, before government-financed construction of three railway trestles at Joggin Bridge, Bear River, and Moose River completed the famous "missing link," joining the two sections of track to provide continuous service. Until then, passengers were forced to find other methods of transportation, typically stagecoach or ferry, to navigate the gaps in rail service. In 1894, the Dominion Atlantic Railway was created through a merger of the two financially strapped, competing railway lines. The first through train under new management made its inaugural run from Yarmouth to Halifax via the Valley on October 1 of that year.

Steam locomotives, such as the one shown here approaching the Bear River bridge, had become dinosaurs by the 1950s and were replaced by diesel engines to move freight, while sleek self-propelled "dayliners" carried passengers. The automobile, long-haul trucking, and worn-out track infrastructure, however, all spelled doom for the railway. Valley stations began closing in the 1970s (some earlier) and many track lines were abandoned by the 1980s. On March 29, 1990, the Dominion Atlantic Railway ceased operations west of Coldbrook on its main track line between Kentville and Yarmouth; everything else shut down within three years.

**TUPPERVILLE
STATION, 1890S**

In the 1890s, there were thirty-one Valley railway stations. As early as August 1956, when postal trucks made their appearance, mail cars were removed from trains and many small stations were no longer needed.

**TAXI DRIVER
LAWRENCE
DURLING (FORE-
GROUND) AWAITS
A FARE AT
BRIDGETOWN
STATION, 1949**

Only four stations survive today. The Bridgetown station has been converted into a pub appropriately named End of the Line. The Middleton station houses Memory Lane Railway Museum, Wolfville's serves as a branch of the Annapolis Valley Regional Library, and the Annapolis Royal station is presently slated for commercial space.

Fear of the unknown can lead to all manner of name calling and dire predictions. So when automobiles made their appearance in the late nineteenth century, various Nova Scotia newspapers labelled them "stink wagons," "running stinkers," "devil wagons," and "gasoline devils." The New Glasgow *Eastern Chronicle* was especially dogged in pillorying the contraptions, claiming in a 1907 editorial of being:

> kept in mortal terror of one of these devil wagons meeting us when we are driving along the road, our horse taking the nearest fence and leaving us stranded on the roadside, possibly maimed for life, and our good looks considerably out of joint... There surely should be some legislation for the people who maintain the roads and who in their daily avocation are constantly called on to use these roads. Their rights should be protected against these life endangering pleasure jaunters...

The first gasoline-powered car in Canada, a one-cylinder Winton, made its appearance in 1898. A year later, William Exshaw, son-in-law of Sir Sandford Flemming (famed railroad architect and "Father of Standard Time"), brought Nova Scotia's inaugural "gasoline horseless carriage" to Halifax by steamer from Liverpool, England. The *Halifax Daily Echo* reported the French-made car "is boxed up but Mr. Exshaw expects to be driving it around the streets in a few days." By 1904, there were six hundred cars in Canada. That same year, Nova Scotia businessmen Archie Pelton and a Mr. Porter of Kentville attended an automobile show in New York City, returning with two Curved Dash Oldsmobiles, the first cars offered for resale in Nova Scotia. By year's end, another fifteen "stink wagons" had been purchased south of the border by Nova Scotians.

In 1907, every automobile owner in Nova Scotia was required by law to pay two dollars and register with the provincial secretary. To William Black of Wolfville goes the honour of being issued the first-ever provincial license plate bearing the number "1" on a plate only three inches high. Sixty-two was the last number given out that year; the number thirteen was skipped for obvious superstitious reasons. Speed limits were also introduced in 1907, the maximum being twelve kilometres an hour in town, nineteen kilometres an hour in a village, and twenty-four kilometres an hour in the countryside.

**RED BRIDGE,
BRIDGETOWN,
C.1910**

Note sign over entrance to bridge: *Keep To The Left & Walk Your Horses Or You Will Be Fined.*

Such a public outcry went up from horse owners with the arrival of automobiles that the following provincial law was introduced in 1907: "The auto must stop on being signalled by raising a hand by a person having in charge a horse or horses, and remain standing until the horses and driver are out of harm's way. Otherwise the rules of the road are observed but if the auto driver is not signalled the burden of care is on him." The general consensus was that horses had no difficulty when approached by a stink wagon head-on but were spooked when surprised from behind with a blast of the horn. A further measure of relief was offered in 1910 when automobiles were banned from Kings and Annapolis County roads on Saturdays and Sundays (Digby County had no such law at the time), with fines ranging from fifty dollars for a first offence to two hundred dollars for a third.

The "Rule of the Road" had always been to keep vehicles of any description to the left of centre as was the custom in Great Britain. A problem arose in 1922, when neighbouring New Brunswick switched to the right in accordance with United States practice but Nova Scotia kept to the left. That meant drivers crossing the border between the two provinces had to switch sides, which caused considerable havoc and several near misses. After four months of mayhem, Nova Scotia finally moved over on April 15, 1923. A humorous story associated with the switch comes from Lunenburg County where 1923 was known as the "Year of Free Beef." Apparently, Lunenburg oxen were not as bright as their Valley kin and couldn't be retrained to move from the left side of the road to the right. This led to their demise as farmers en masse were forced to train new teams, with the "slow-witted" old guard ending up as table fare, knocking the bottom out of beef market prices in the county.

DETOUR FOR ROAD PAVING AT BRIDGETOWN, 1949

In 1918, there were forty-six thousand cars in Canada, 1,435 of them in Nova Scotia. Within five years, the number increased to eighteen thousand. Wolfville had Nova Scotia's first paved main street in 1912, but not until the 1930s were there paved provincial highways. In 1908, Nova Scotia had 28,800 kilometres of gravel highway. By 1933, there were only thirty kilometres of paved road; in 1940, it had jumped to 1,600 kilometres. Driving during the early years was mostly a summer touring pastime. Mud-clogged, rutted roads in spring were a deterrent to any form of travel; the *Hants Journal* in April 1925 announced, "The highways are to remain closed to motor vehicles until the first day of June." Cost of maintaining highways in 1915 was $5.75 a kilometre; ten years later a gasoline tax was introduced for the upkeep of roads. By 1933, there was one gasoline pump for every seventeen registered automobiles in Canada, but in Nova Scotia there was one pump for every ten automobiles. Richard Harris of Aylesford opened the province's first full service garage in the mid-1920s, Aylesford Service and Filling Station, offering to clean windshields and check oil (until then garages only pumped gas). This was such a success he opened the Wolfville Park Filling Station in 1927. With improved roads, a greater number of automobile tourists began arriving, steadily increasing from two thousand in 1922 to nearly fifty thousand in 1940. A report for 1962 shows 15,178 Massachusetts automobiles touring Nova Scotia, followed by New York with 7,804. The average American tourist stayed 9.92 days and spent $9.77 per day; Canadian tourists (who made up 67% of traffic) stayed 11.09 days and spent $6.30 per day.

Chapter 3

Land of Evangeline

Greetings from

ANNAPOLIS RIVER, N.S.

1922 POSTCARD

During the early 1900s, hundreds of images taken by Valley photographers such as Ralph Harris, Paul Yates, Lewis Rice, A. L. Hardy, and Edson Graham were turned into postcards such as this, depicting pastoral settings, scenic vistas, and streetscapes.

"Land of Evangeline" is a collage of postcards and photographs which focuses on selected points of interest from Digby to Windsor. Except for the occasional detour, the reader travels Highway 1, the highway that for much of the twentieth century served as the main route connecting Yarmouth and Halifax. In recent years Highway 1 has been relegated to secondary road status with the completion of Highway 101. Born from a necessity to accommodate increasing demands of society, the speedy thoroughfare bypasses the soul of the Valley. Only by taking the time to explore Highway 1 and its many off-shoots can one gain an appreciation for what makes the Valley a special place.

CANADIAN PACIFIC RAILWAY PINES HOTEL, DIGBY, 1932

In the late 1890s, the Valley was well served by steamship service with the Dominion Atlantic Railway operating ferries from Yarmouth to Boston, Digby to Saint John, and Kingsport to Parrsboro. Yarmouth was advertised as the "Gateway to Nova Scotia" for Americans from the eastern seaboard who comprised the majority of tourist trade at that time. By 1912, the Yarmouth to Boston run was under the control of Eastern Steam Ship Corporation, a Canadian Pacific Railway subsidiary. A year later, the C. P. R. acquired running rights on the Dominion Atlantic Railway tracks for 999 years, taking over its Digby to Saint John ferry service and Minas Basin route between Parrsboro, Kingsport, and Wolfville but leaving the D. A. R. name for the railway side of operations. During the gilded age of transcontinental train travel which began in the late nineteenth century, the Canadian Pacific Railway acquired the Pines Hotel at Digby in 1917-1918 to complete its coast-to-coast chain of opulent resorts. Originally a small, privately owned wooden hotel built in 1903, the CPR replaced it in 1929 with this Norman chateau-style design. A similar railway hotel, Lakeside Inn, was opened two years later outside Yarmouth on Lake Milo. In addition to ease of access from Yarmouth and Digby for a burgeoning New England tourist market, the Valley held an ace-in-the-hole over the rest of Nova Scotia. The Americans had a fascination for Longfellow's 1847 poem *Evangeline* which railway and steamship promotional literature played up to the fullest. Scores of booklets, brochures, and articles from 1885 through the 1930s made reference to the fictitious maiden—*Nova Scotia, the Land of Evangeline and the Tourist's Paradise; The Evangeline Souvenir Album; Acadian Land In Nova Scotia: The Evangeline Country*. A 1928 Kingsport and Parrsboro steamship advertisement emphasized "The most popular line of travel to the American, Canadian, and European tourist desirous of making acquaintance with the picturesque scenery, varied resources and health-giving air of Nova Scotia, is that so well-known as the 'Land of Evangeline' Route."

THIS IS THE BOAT THAT BROUGHT ME TO THE MYRTLE HOTEL, DIGBY, NOVA SCOTIA

C. P. R. FERRY ARRIVING AT DIGBY, EARLY 1900S

In 1918, Digby had twenty hotels and boarding houses catering to tourists. As early as 1826, Bay of Fundy steamship service was operational between New Brunswick and Nova Scotia. Until the 1890s, Annapolis Royal was the terminal point on the Saint John-Digby-Annapolis Royal route. With completion of the railway in 1891, Digby became the only port-of-call for the Bay of Fundy ferry, a role it fills to this day.

Railroad Photo Studio.

BRIDGETOWN'S GRANVILLE STREET, LATE 1800S

Photographers were often hired by railway companies to produce enticing images for tourist advertising purposes. In some cases, private rail cars served as travelling studios. Lewis Rice was one noted Valley photographer with studios in Windsor and Wolfville who produced photographs from a railway car.

Digby's claim to fame for more than two centuries has been its fishery. Smoked herring (Digby chickens), smoked haddock (finnan haddie), dried cod, hake and pollock, fresh and frozen halibut, clams, winkles, mussels, lobsters, and scallops have all found their way into worldwide markets over the years. The lobster in this Paul Yates photograph was pinned to a sheet of wood, the white backdrop giving the illusion of Agate casually holding the giant crustacean by his fingertips. Prior to the 1800s, lobster was considered a poor man's meal, often washing ashore into piles almost a metre high. Legend has it that an eighteenth-century British naval captain at Halifax sent his steward to the city market with a sovereign ($2.40) to buy lobster for the evening meal and received three wheelbarrow loads in return. Today's market lobster are canners compared to the behemoths of yore when forty pounders were commonplace. The world's biggest lobster, according to the *Guinness Book of Records,* was caught off the coast of Nova Scotia in 1977, weighing in at 20.14 kilograms (44 pounds, 6 ounces) and measuring 1.06 metres (3 feet, 6 inches) from tail-fan to the tip of the largest claw. It is left to the reader to speculate how much this Digby lobster weighed and the price it fetched, given that fishermen were paid six cents a pound, the going rate until 1922.

DIGBY SCALLOP FLEET

When the commercial scallop fishery began in the 1920s, the mollusk delicacies, like lobsters, were considerably larger than today's cousins, with only six or eight needed to make a pound. Sold initially by the gallon and shipped in barrels by train to the United States, when the unit of measurement switched in the 1930s, scallops fetched eight cents a pound. Digby had the world's largest scallop fleet—eighty to ninety boats—by the 1950s, and it accounted for ninety percent of Canada's scallop catch. Fishermen were paid forty cents a pound at dockside.

DIGBY TOURIST BUREAU

Note the tourist information bureau sign over the garage door. The forerunner of today's private sector tourism organizations began in 1897 with the establishment of the Nova Scotia Tourist Association at Halifax. In the 1930s, there was the Land of Evangeline Tourist Association at Annapolis Royal. The provincial government entered the picture in 1924, setting up the Tourist Investigation Committee (now the Department of Tourism) which evolved into the Bureau of Information & Publicity in 1930 under the Minister of Highways, which may explain having the tourist bureau in a garage.

MOUNTAIN GAP INN, SMITH'S COVE, DIGBY COUNTY, 1925

With its breathtaking scenery of the Annapolis Basin, close proximity to the Digby-Saint John ferry, and direct access to the Dominion Atlantic Railway, Smith's Cove was a summer home to American tourists by the 1880s. A number of boarding houses and hotels have come and gone since then. Two still in operation are Mountain Gap Inn (above) and Harbourview Hotel and Log Cabin Colony (right). Mountain Gap Inn's original owner, Ernest Alma Thornton, was a travelling salesman for Fraser Thornton Ltd., a Cookshire, Quebec company that manufactured patent medicines in the early 1900s. Digby County was part of his sales circuit and in 1915, Thornton purchased property at Smith's Cove where he took up residency and continued to market various medicinal products including Olivine Emulsion (cod liver oil) and Syrup of Tar and Codeine, a cough suppressant for chronic bronchitis and tuberculosis. How Thornton became involved in tourism is unclear but he was widely noted for "marketing aggressiveness"—a necessary trait for a man in his line of work. Pharmaceutical sales and inn keeping were a lucrative combination as local sources claimed he was the only resident of Smith's Cove in the 1920s and 1930s wealthy enough to pay income tax. Mountain Gap today features 107 units including some of the original buildings and claims to be the oldest privately owned resort in Nova Scotia.

Patrons of neighbouring Harbourview Hotel and Log Cabin Colony could step off the D. A. R. a mere one hundred metres from the front door. Owner William Cossaboom advertised his establishment in 1924 as:

> distinctly different from any other resort in Canada. From its inception [1900] a carefully exercised policy of soliciting only the most desirable class of patrons has resulted in an entire colony of people with whom it is a pleasure—even an honour—to associate… You may build your own cabin, or the management will build one for you at surprisingly low cost. Cabins fully furnished with bath and electric lights, may be rented for the season but should be engaged a year in advance. The central dining room accommodates 200 guests. The proprietor takes pride in supplying the freshest vegetables, cream, fruit, fish and farm products obtainable in a country rich in fertile farms and noted for the delicacy and fine flavor of its seafood… Service characterized by a genuine good will and hospitality, without ostentation, and by a consistent endeavor to provide every home-like comfort and attention desired.

HARBOURVIEW HOTEL & LOG CABIN COLONY, C.1920

RELAXING IN ONE OF HARBOURVIEW'S THIRTY COTTAGES, C.1946

ANNAPOLIS COUNTY SIDE OF BEAR RIVER, C.1912

DIGBY COUNTY SIDE OF BEAR RIVER, C.1909

Bear River is unique in that the river, which bisects the village and empties into the Annapolis Basin six kilometres away, serves as the municipal line between Annapolis and Digby Counties. At the height of its prosperity in the late nineteenth century, Bear River boasted five shipyards, a steamship company, customs house, eleven general stores, numerous specialty shops and craftsmen, a dentist and two doctors, a telegraph and telephone office, newspaper, and electric power plant. Nine roads converged on the village where as many as seven vessels at one time were tied to its wharves loading butter, eggs, apples, cherries, and ten million feet of lumber annually for shipment to Saint John, Boston, New York and the Caribbean. Clinging to the steep slopes of the South Upland, Bear River has long been publicized as the "Switzerland of Nova Scotia."

TWELVE KILOMETRES EAST OF BEAR RIVER IS CLEMENTSPORT, SHOWN HERE FROM THE RAILWAY BRIDGE, EARLY 1900S.

ONE OF THE "MISSING LINKS" AT MOOSE RIVER

Calnek described Clementsport as "very prettily situated in a sort of ravine through which the [Moose] river finds its way to the Annapolis River which it enters through a large tidal mouth of sufficient depth to admit large-sized vessels." Today, a commemorative cairn near the bridge attests to Clementsport's seafaring days. It lists fourteen master mariners, all named Rawding, beginning with Joseph Rawding in 1771. Dedicated in 1964, the inscription reads: "These sea captains, all resident in the locality and members of the one family, roamed the Seven Seas for 150 years and had under their command some of the largest vessels then existing." The small coastal steam packet shown passing through the swing section of railroad trestle was typical of those used in the Bay of Fundy until the early 1900s to carry freight and passengers. The railway bridge was one of three mentioned earlier built by the Federal Government in 1891 to complete the "Missing Link," which until then had prevented continuous train service through the Valley.

**EDWARD PHINLEY
MORSE MANSION
"TRAIL'S END,"
DEEP BROOK, 1942**

Edward Phinley Morse (1859-1930) of Clementsport began his career apprenticing at a Yarmouth shipyard forge in 1878, then moved to New England in search of employment where he eventually became head of the world's largest shipbuilding and drydock firm. In 1934, Morse Dry Dock Company of South Brooklyn, New York, merged with five other dry dock companies to form United Dry Docks Ltd. of which E. P. Morse was president. During the spring and summer months he returned to Clementsport with his wife Ada Martha (née Gavel: born in Tusket in 1860, died in Clementsport in 1947) where he maintained a vacation home known as "The Hermitage." In 1929, Morse purchased four hundred acres of ancestral land on Morton's Point in neighbouring Deep Brook, renamed it Morse's Point, and in June of the following year began building a $250,000 retirement residence he called "Trail's End." Unfortunately he never lived to see it completed. While visiting the work site in August 1930, he suffered a fatal heart attack at the gateway. The *Weekly Monitor* of August 27, 1930, reported: "The return of the Clementsport boy giving employment to so many men and developing and restoring landmarks was hailed with delight here, and his sudden passing is a matter of sincere regret by countless friends who mourn the loss of a most esteemed citizen." The details of his will made for juicy gossip in the *Weekly Monitor* of October 1, 1930:

> It disposed of an estate estimated at almost $40 million to his widow, two children and [seven] grandchildren and cut off without a cent his son Edward P. Morse with whom he had quarrelled over business matters… He made provisions for the son's children however although their shares amount to less than those of other grand children. Ten years ago, Edward P. Morse Jr. sued his father for the recovery of certain profits alleged to be his due under an agreement whereby the son became general manager of his father's drydock plant.

"Trail's End" remained unfinished and vacant until World War II when the federal government purchased the land and buildings in 1942 for twenty-six thousand dollars and incorporated it into HMCS Cornwallis, converting the house into an officers' mess, the servants' quarters for the Captain's home, the stables and garage into offices, and the coach house for the Protestant Padre's Married Quarters.

As Allied losses to German U-boats mounted in World War II, and Canada's role fighting the Battle of the Atlantic expanded, HMCS Cornwallis was commissioned at Halifax May 1, 1942, to train much-needed personnel for the Royal Canadian Navy. Dockyard space allotted for the facility, however, was inadequate as well as urgently needed for wartime logistical reasons. The decision was made to build a new, larger training base elsewhere. Shelburne along the south shore was initially chosen but Deep Brook on the Annapolis Basin won out, a political decision many feel was influenced by J. L. Ilsley, the MP for Digby, Annapolis and Kings counties and a powerful member of Prime Minister Mackenzie King's cabinet. Thousands of tradesmen were employed building the nine-million-dollar base and in April 1943, Cornwallis was officially transferred from Halifax to Deep Brook. It opened with a complement of 2,539 men but was quickly brought up to speed after which there were never less than eleven thousand trainees and instructors (men and women) until war's end. Courses lasted only six to eight weeks as time was of the essence with ships needing crews. HMCS Cornwallis contributed immeasurably to Canada possessing the world's third largest navy by 1945, the majority of its nearly one hundred thousand personnel passing through the training base. Cornwallis served as a discharge transit centre following the war, then was declared surplus and turned over to War Assets for disposal in 1946, but was re-commissioned in 1949 with growing world tension over events in Korea. The facility remained operational (and an economic mainstay of the area) for another forty-six years, changing from HMCS Cornwallis to CFB (Canadian Forces Base) Cornwallis in 1968 with the unification of Canada's army, navy, and air force. At that time, it became the Canadian Forces recruit training school for all English-speaking members of the three armed forces with St. Jean, Quebec, serving the equivalent role for French-speaking recruits. Cornwallis filled a variety of training roles until political cutbacks led to its official closure in May 1995; members of "new entry training course #9426" were its last graduates on August 18, 1994. Once the largest naval training facility in the British Commonwealth and having graduated five hundred thousand personnel in fifty-one years, the base now serves as an industrial park, sea cadet summer training facility, and the Lester B. Pearson Peacekeeping Centre.

THE MOOSELAND TRAIL

Pictured above is Lequille, near Annapolis Royal. By the 1860s, a stagecoach road through Lequille connected Annapolis Royal with Liverpool 112 kilometres away on Nova Scotia's south shore. In the early 1900s, this route was touted in advertising brochures as the "Mooseland Trail" for summer tourists staying at hotels, camps, and private lodges in the backcountry of Annapolis and Queens counties. The period from 1871 to 1940 has been categorized by Dr. James Morrison of Saint Mary's University as the "elite sport tourist" era in Nova Scotia. He picked 1871 as being especially significant because it was during July of that year a party of four hundred Bostonians arrived in Nova Scotia by train via New Brunswick, the first "tourist excursion" of its kind. Within a year, New Yorkers could reach the province by rail in a mere thirty-six hours, leaving behind the "wilds of New York City [for] the civilized wilderness of Nova Scotia." Some who came later were outdoor writers such as Albert Bigelow Paine whose 1908 classic, *The Tent Dwellers,* spoke glowingly of the unspoiled beauty afforded by Annapolis County and the angler's delight in catching trout "as big as your leg." Such tales drew widespread attention south of the border where much of the forest land was being stripped bare. By 1911, trains were bringing in 1,800 American tourists a week with many others arriving by ferries. Unlike post-World War II summer visitors who toured the province in automobiles and stayed for short periods of time (giving rise to the "mobile tourist era"), those of the "elite sport tourist" period came with trunks and bags in hand, prepared to plunk themselves down for two months or more; many became fixtures in a community and returned year after year. Easily reached by rail and ferry, Annapolis Royal was a popular destination for those making connections with the "Mooseland Trail" which led to the famed sporting grounds of Milford, Kejimkujik and Lake Rossignol. Buckboards, then trucks later on, met travellers in town and transported them fifty kilometres or more over a tortuous rutted road to inns like Milford House or private members' retreats such as Kedgemakooge Rod & Gun Club. The arduous trip may explain in part why tourists stayed all summer. According to Dr. Morrison, local residents were "never altogether clear as to why this rich crowd would want to spend $10 a week for board just to sit around an oil lamp in the wilds of Nova Scotia."

ANNAPOLIS ROYAL LOOKING FROM FORT ANNE TOWARD GEORGE STREET

This 1930s picture was made into a postcard by photographer Paul Yates. With a population of only 550 in 2004 (compared to just 959 in 1891), Annapolis Royal is proof that size doesn't matter. Arguably the birthplace of Canada, the immediate area was colonized by settlers two years before Jamestown, Virginia, three years before Quebec, and fifteen years before the Pilgrims dropped anchor at Plymouth, Massachusetts. Popular with summer tourists, part of the town has been designated a National Historic District.

GRANVILLE FERRY

Directly across the river from Annapolis Royal is the village of Granville Ferry, seen here in a late 1890s photo of Main Street that also was turned into a souvenir postcard. Granville Ferry is said to have been more prosperous than Annapolis Royal in the mid-1800s. Ferries plied back and forth between the two communities from at least 1777 until 1921 when a bridge was finally completed over the river.

AUTHOR MARTHA
BANNING THOMAS
STANDS IN FRONT
OF FUNDY VIEW
TOURIST HOUSE &
COTTAGES,
VICTORIA BEACH,
1949

A detour of thirty kilometres at Granville Ferry takes one along the north side of the Annapolis Basin to Victoria Beach, described by an early traveller as a "scenic toy fishing village perched precariously at the edge of a cliff." Situated on the east shore of the "Gut" directly across from the town of Digby, it was here in 1849 that Nova Scotia Pony Express riders from Halifax carrying packets of the latest European news for Boston and New York rendezvoused with steamers bound for the telegraph offices of Saint John, New Brunswick. The venture was short-lived, however, terminating after only eight months when the telegraph was extended from Saint John to Halifax.

More than seventy years ago, Mrs. John Casey opened Fundy View House and Cottages, a summer tourist retreat still operated by her son Joe Casey, a well-known local businessman and politician. A noteworthy but seldom heard of visitor to Victoria Beach in the early years was Martha Banning Thomas (1888-1968), an American-born writer who spent many summers at Fundy View House before purchasing a cottage and living full-time in the village for twenty years during the mid-1900s. Often writing under the pseudonym Patience Eden or Calvin George, her short stories and verse appeared in a host of magazines and newspapers including *Maclean's, Chatelaine, Saturday Evening Post, New York Times* and *New York Herald Tribune.* In 1936, her novel *Stormalong Gert* was published in the United States by McGraw Hill; John Lane of London, England, also printed the book under the title *A Woman of the Sea.* Hollywood showed interest in basing a movie on the manuscript's lead character but production plans never materialized. Thomas counted many distinguished American and Canadian personalities among her friends and visitors to Victoria Beach, including Nova Scotians Thomas Raddall, Helen Creighton, and Dr. Watson Kirkconnell. She once wrote of her adopted province, "I love Nova Scotia. There is a certain quality of land and people which, once it gets under your skin—you are an inhabitant. You both ache and sing with its beauty."

GATHERING DULSE AT VICTORIA BEACH WITH DIGBY GUT IN BACKGROUND, 1940S

LAYING DULSE OUT TO DRY

Dulse (*Palmaria palmata*) is a reddish-purple coloured seaweed found in the North Atlantic and Northwest Pacific which grows on rocks in the intertidal zone—the area between low and high tide. Harvest is from June to September when it is handpicked at low tide, then spread out along beaches, fields and roadways to dry. In Atlantic Canada there are only two kinds of dulse, that which grows around Grand Manan Island, New Brunswick, and the dulse found at Victoria Beach. Regional biases aside, market demand for both is high. Rich in dietary nutrients, dulse is claimed to fight a host of infections and illnesses. To savour dulse is an acquired taste, as its unique, intense tang can be an affront to the first timer's palate. All is not lost, however, because the "sea vegetable" is also diced, chopped, fried, spread, and dissolved into a variety of soups, stews, chowders, casseroles, and salads.

**TURNIP BARN,
GRANVILLE
CENTRE**

Three kilometres east of Annapolis Royal along Highway 1 at Granville Centre stands an architectural oddity known as the "Troop Barn" or "Turnip Barn." There are different stories as to how William B. Troop, a descendant of New England Planters, came to build the barn in 1888. According to one, he saw an octagonal (eight-sided) barn while visiting friends in New Brunswick. Upon returning home, he is said to have taken a large turnip from the garden and carved out a model for carpenters to work from, thus the nickname Turnip Barn. Another source attributes the barn's design to a book Troop read that was written by Orson Squire Fowler (1809-1889), a renowned New York City phrenologist. (Webster's Dictionary defines "phrenology" as "the study of the conformation of the skull based on the belief that it is indicative of mental faculties and character.") In 1848, Fowler published *A Home For All* in which he touted the advantages to be had from building octagonal houses. He used mathematics to prove his point that octagons are one-fifth larger inside than a four-sided house of comparable size and they were cheaper to build and cut down on heat loss. He also claimed that octagons permitted the entry of more light and provided better ventilation in summer. Fowler was not proposing anything radically new, just popularizing a concept that had been around since the 1650s in the eastern United States. Thomas Jefferson designed more than fifty buildings incorporating octagonal features and Mark Twain penned *Tom Sawyer* and *Huckleberry Finn* while squirrelled away in an octagonal study designed after a riverboat captain's cabin. Following the release of Fowler's book, hundreds of octagonal buildings from houses to outhouses were built in the United States. Embraced in Ontario as well, the octagon never caught on in Nova Scotia. An occasional one turned up, like the so-called Ink Bottle House in Dartmouth which was built in 1871 but torn down in the late 1900s to make way for an apartment high-rise. Today, Troop's octagon barn is privately owned and a designated Nova Scotia heritage building.

PARKER HOUSE, BELLEISLE

Five kilometres east of Granville Centre on the Belleisle Marsh is a second but less conspicuous heritage landmark. The Parker House, dating to 1791, is the oldest brick house in Annapolis County and one of the earliest in Nova Scotia. The marsh was named in 1667 for Le Sieur de Belleisle who was granted ownership as part of his seigneury when he took command of Port Royal following the Treaty of Breda. In 1765, New England Planters moved into the Granville Township, one of whom was Abijah Parker from Connecticut. Parker received a land grant of two five-hundred-acre parcels that stretched from the bank of the Annapolis River up and over the North Mountain to the Bay of Fundy. In the Valley near a brook overlooking the Belleisle Marsh he built a house, some say upon an old Acadian foundation, and thereafter made a successful life lumbering and farming. When Abijah died in 1780, the property passed to his son Obadiah. He went back to Boston at some point to learn the finer points of the building trade, and upon his return, began work on this brick house in 1791 that incorporated a part of his father's old homestead. Parker House was well put together, with double brick walls sixteen inches thick and floor planks measuring twenty-three inches in width. It is believed the bricks were hand-made on site from readily available clay, which was pressed into wooden moulds and then fired in a kiln. The work was tediously slow, taking approximately six years to complete because only so many courses of brick could be laid in any given year due to slow-drying lime mortar. The house was renovated somewhat in 1830, with the end chimneys removed and two central ones installed to accommodate newly introduced stoves. The dormer is not original to the house and what once was the back door is now the front, facing onto Highway 1. The farm remained in the Parker family for many years. In 1882, W. D. Almon Parker sold the house, including part of the land, and built a larger residence with higher ceilings across the road. Apparently, at six feet two inches tall, he had tired of thumping his head against low door frames. Listed on the Canadian Inventory of Historical Buildings, the Parker house is privately owned today.

John Quirk, who it is said owned half the houses in Bridgetown, operated this building as the Golden Ball Inn from 1828 to 1889. Later known as Quirk's Hotel and then used as a grocery store at the time of this 1890s photo, the landmark was torn down around 1900. Bridgetown today is a quiet, immaculate community with elm-treed streets and stately Victorian homes. The population remains relatively unchanged from one hundred years ago. In 1891, it stood at 1,117; the census of 2001 reported 1,035. Advertised as the "prettiest little town in Nova Scotia," it has received little historical fanfare compared to other Valley towns like Digby, Annapolis Royal, Kentville, Wolfville, and Windsor, but at one time Bridgetown was a beehive of industrial and commercial activity. When Digby County was formed in 1837 from subdividing Annapolis County, a thirty-year squabble ensued between Annapolis Royal and Bridgetown as to which should be shiretown for the newly aligned Annapolis County. A truce was finally declared in 1870 when the Nova Scotia Legislative Council stepped in and passed an act splitting civic duties between the communities.

Lovell's 1873 *Gazetteer of British North America* described Bridgetown as a "flourishing post village which possesses excellent water power and contains an iron foundry, a tannery, several stores and hotels, a telegraph office, and a printing office issuing a weekly newspaper." (*Western News: the Kings, Annapolis and Digby Weekly Gazette* begun in 1856, was the first newspaper in Annapolis County.) Mention was made earlier of Bridgetown's importance as a shipbuilding centre and port of entry. Further to that, county historian W. A. Calnek writes, "From being at the head of river navigation, it immediately developed an export trade, [for] the products of all the valley eastward of it and the mountains north and south." In 1879, three packets were making regular runs during summer months to Boston and Saint John. Tourist excursion boats from Digby's numerous hotels sailed up the Annapolis River to Bridgetown, arriving and departing with the tides.

J. H. Hicks & Sons was the town's largest and most diversified business venture in the early 1900s, advertising itself as builders, contractors, manufacturers, undertakers, and embalmers. The Hicks family has a long, distinguished history of civic mindedness starting with John, who represented Granville from 1768-1770 in the Provincial House of Assembly. Henry B. Hicks (1879-1951) served three terms as mayor of Bridgetown while his son, the Hon. Henry D. Hicks (1915-1990) was premier of Nova Scotia (1954-1956), president of Dalhousie University (1963-1980), and Parliamentary senator (1972-1990).

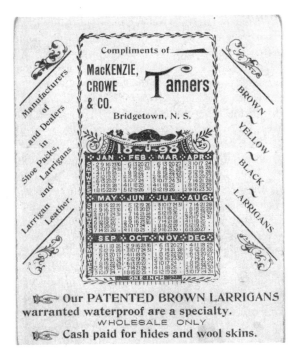

Footwear was a valuable commodity. In 1772, tanner Jacob Troop purchased a farm lot near Granville Ferry, financing it with four hundred pairs of adult shoes which he promised to deliver over four years. MacKenzie, Crowe & Co., who operated in Bridgetown from 1880-1918, was one of fifty-two Annapolis County businesses in the 1890s tanning hides and turning them into leather goods. The two proprietors, possibly standing front and centre, displayed business acumen, having this stiff cardboard stock advertisement produced, copies of which were likely distributed to patrons much as calendars are today.

Unlike many communities that were economically stagnating by the mid-1900s, Bridgetown expanded upon old business ventures and enticed new ones. One of these began in the late 1890s as the Annapolis Valley Cyder Company (above). Details are sketchy but it appears the original bottling plant was opened by Ronald Whiteway from England to produce apple cider vinegar. Minard Graves (a Valley industrialist who built his reputation upon apples and about whom more will be said in later chapters), purchased Whiteway's business in 1920 and began manufacturing Evangeline brand soft drinks. That same year, C. L. Grigg of St. Louis launched his Howdy Orange drink. Grigg then went on to develop a new "refreshing and thirst-quenching" beverage introduced in 1929 as "Bib-Label Lithiated Lemon-Lime Soda," a lengthy handle soon shortened to Seven-Up. (As a side note, Seven-Up originally contained small amounts of lithium and was marketed in the prohibition era as a cure for hangovers). Grigg changed the name of his business from The Howdy Corporation to The Seven-Up Company in 1936, and by the late 1940s, Seven-Up was the third best selling soft drink in the world. Back in Bridgetown, Minard Graves at some point during that period of time entered a franchise agreement for Seven-Up and Nesbitt's Orange drinks under the name Seven-Up Maritimes Ltd. Business was brisk, with Evangeline trucks delivering soft drinks from one end of the province to the other; by 1949, seven bottling plants were operating throughout the Maritimes. Following a fire at the Bridgetown plant in 1951, a new building was erected near the train station. In 1960, the business was sold to Sussex Beverages (of Golden Ginger Ale fame) in New Brunswick. On January 24, 1973, the *Bridgetown Monitor* carried a front page headline announcing, "Seven-Up, Sussex Closes Doors." Again under new ownership, this time Jones Bottling Company, the plant's name was changed for the last time to Maritime Beverages, a Saint John, New Brunswick, company. Where Evangeline had once employed fifteen full-time workers at Bridgetown, and many others during summer months, new management turned the plant into a warehouse with only a shipper and two salesmen; shortly after, it was closed down.

EVANGELINE SOFT DRINKS PRODUCED AND DISTRIBUTED BY ANNAPOLIS VALLEY CYDER COMPANY LTD., BRIDGETOWN, C.1941.

FLEET OF EVANGELINE DELIVERY TRUCKS, BRIDGETOWN, C.1941

ACADIAN DISTILLERY, BRIDGETOWN, c.1960

In 1951, L. J. McGuinness Co. Ltd. from Toronto purchased a vacant Bridgetown fruit-processing plant from Minard Graves and converted it into the first distillery east of Montreal. The *Bridgetown Monitor* called the move "an economically sound idea" in light of the fact Nova Scotians at the time quaffed more rum per capita than any province in Canada (perhaps stemming from a long seafaring tradition). The newspaper spoke glowingly of natural advantages the Valley afforded for such a business venture. "Of prime importance in the location of a distillery is the atmosphere, humidity, temperature, amount of sunshine, absence of smog—all have a bearing on the quality of the product. Whiskey and rum breathe as they mature. The type of air it has to breathe reflects directly on its flavour and quality. The purity of the water is another factor directly affecting any distillate." Bridgetown had "all the favourable climatic conditions." Aside from the obvious infusion of jobs and tax revenues, the point was emphasized that farmers would benefit twofold—by growing grains required for production and having the opportunity to feed "spent" grain to their cattle, which was claimed to produce a higher grade of beef. Initial plans called for bottling a mixture of imported West Indies rum with rum produced on site. Within a short time, however, the plant was manufacturing a variety of rum, whiskey, gin, vodka, brandy, and wine that was sold in Atlantic Canada and Quebec. Several expansions followed; in 1964, a fifteen-thousand-barrel warehouse was built followed by a forty-thousand-barrel warehouse in 1970 (before marketing, rum was aged four years; whiskey three, five, eight, and twelve years). A two-million-dollar upgrade in 1969 included a new bottling plant with three production lines, one capable of filling 120 to 180 bottles per minute. McGuinness, in business since 1904 and operating plants across the country, claimed to be the only one hundred percent family-owned Canadian distillery. In 1970, they sold the Bridgetown operation to Standard Brands, which continued operating the plant until 1986, when it—along with one-quarter of the world's distilleries—was closed during a massive downsizing, the result of a shift from "production-driven to market-driven" business philosophy.

PRODUCING ELASTIC THREAD, UNITED ELASTIC LIMITED, BRIDGETOWN, 1960s

For the better part of fifty years, a tower 180 feet tall topped with a red and white steel ball served as a landmark for people travelling between Bridgetown and Annapolis Royal. The water storage tank, now a rusting sphere, looms over the vacant three-acre factory that once was the largest manufacturer of elastic fabrics in Canada. In 1959, a Massachusetts firm built the United Elastic plant to the west of Bridgetown on the south side of the Annapolis River at Centrelea; similar plants were built at the time in Belgium and Mexico. United Elastic of Bridgetown manufactured a variety of products for thirty Canadian industries. Business boomed and several expansions were carried out between 1964 and 1974. In the late 1960s, textile giant J. P. Stevens & Co. Inc. of New York took over ownership at which time the Belgian plant was closed. On July 3, 1980, the Bridgetown plant was abruptly shut down, putting 160 people out of work. The decision was undoubtedly influenced by tremendous pressure exerted upon the company by U. S. textile workers, politicians, civil rights leaders, church groups and other parties who organized a 1976 national boycott of J. P. Stevens products in response to decades of alleged labour law violations. The battle gained global attention, fueled by the 1979 Oscar-winning movie *Norma Rae*. A concerted effort was made to save the Bridgetown plant by organizing workers into a cooperative which took on ownership under the new name of Britex. By 1999, nearly 240 people were employed and export markets had been expanded into Hong Kong, Sri Lanka, and Australia. Mounting debt and the loss of ninety percent of the U. S. market to cross-border trade disputes, however, resulted in its labour force being cut in half by 2003. In September 2004, the plant was closed and its equipment auctioned off. The Valley's single largest industrial manufacturer today is Michelin North America (Canada) Inc. which built a tire manufacturing plant (one of three in Nova Scotia) at Waterville, Kings County, in 1982 and currently provides employment for 1,100 people.

DR. WILLIAM INGLIS MORSE, 1934

William Inglis Morse is known as the "millionaire preacher." Born in 1874 at Paradise, Annapolis County, Morse began his studies for the ministry at Acadia University (B.A. 1897), then went on to the Episcopal Theological School, in Cambridge, Massachusetts (B.D. 1900). He was ordained a Deacon in Ministry of the Episcopal Church in 1900 and a priest the following year. Morse taught at Westminister School in Simsbury, Connecticut (1900-1902), served as curator of St. John's Church, Standford, Connecticut (1902-1905), and was rector of the Church of the Incarnation, in Lynn, Massachusetts (1905-1929). He received two honourary degrees, one in 1926 from Acadia University (D. Litt.), the other in 1939 from Dalhousie University (L.L.D.). Despite his early theological leanings, Morse is said to have dedicated his life after 1930 to conducting historical research on Nova Scotia and eastern New England. None of his training or work experience explains why he is remembered as the "millionaire preacher." That in all likelihood stems from 1904 when he married Susan Alice Ensign from Simsbury, Connecticut, the daughter of a wealthy industrialist possibly connected to the Ensign Manufacturing Company which built, among many things, railroad cars of all types. Whatever the family origin, there's little question William hit the jackpot. In 1917, the couple established a summer home at Paradise on the Morse ancestral land which they named "Pansy Patch" for "endless rows of pansies in the expansive gardens." That same year, he sunk fifty thousand dollars into a "crude" golf course on his four-hundred-acre estate which he predictably named Pansy Patch Golf Club; this formed the basis for the original nine hole Eden Golf Club (now eighteen holes) which was built between 1940 and 1944. Morse went on to become a prolific writer and collector of rare books and autographed letters which today are housed in collections at Acadia, Dalhousie, and Harvard Universities. As just one example of his acquisitions, on a European trip in 1931 he purchased a 1487 edition of Dante's *Divina Commedia* from dealers in Naples, then had to smuggle it out of Europe wrapped either in a rubber blanket or medicine chest. The Morses had one child, a daughter, Susan Toy (born in 1905) who married Frederick W. Hilles, an English professor at Yale. William Morse passed away on his birthday, June 4, 1952, just five days shy of the first anniversary marking his wife's death. The October 25, 1963, issue of the Halifax *Chronicle Herald* carried a detailed account of Mrs. Frederick Hilles giving Pansy Patch to the provincial government. Included with the estate were three residences, one of which Mrs. Hilles was to retain use of so long as she lived. Mention was made in the newspaper article that Pansy Patch was one of seven estates owned by William Morse in the Paradise and Lawrencetown area. The property today is administered in part by the Nova Scotia Department of Social Services which conducts residential summer programs at "Camp Hilles" for adults with special needs.

Phil Milo (centre), a teacher at the Land Survey School, supervises students Ola Laveque (left) and Joseph Cormier using a Geodimeter, the "remarkable new instrument" for measuring distance with light waves. The story of how a village the size of Lawrencetown (population 787 in 1956) became home for what today is the internationally recognized College of Geographic Sciences can only be described as unusual. It all hinged upon two men who never met or even knew the other existed but shared the same vision.

Dr. James Barclay Hall (1843-1928) was born at Lawrencetown. Nestled midway between Bridgetown and Middleton, Calnek writes of the community in 1897, "Lawrencetown with its three churches, gang-saw-mill, carding and grist mills, its bridge and railway station, added to its situation in the midst of productive orchards and well-tilled farms, is altogether a pleasant village, and a very desirable place of residence." Dr. Hall eventually went on to become a widely travelled and noted academic who, in his will, bequeathed a substantial endowment for the establishment of a vocational school in Annapolis County.

Major James Church (1883-1967) was born in India, and immigrated to Canada in 1902. He served with the Royal Engineers during World War I, and then retired with his wife to Lawrencetown at the age of only forty-seven to become a "gentleman farmer." Why he chose Lawrencetown is anyone's guess; perhaps he read Calnek's county history. When World War II erupted, Major Church came out of retirement and, being too old for overseas duty, was delegated to organize No. 6 Vocational Training School (Canadian Army) at the Nova Scotia Technical College in Halifax. At war's end, he was appointed head of the Provincial Land Survey Course, a Canadian Vocational Training Program for veterans. Successful in convincing bureaucrats that a rural setting was more beneficial than Halifax for practical field studies, Major Church transferred the course in 1946 to Lawrencetown. After moving between Lawrencetown and Middleton for a few years, the Land Survey School (better known then as Major Church's School) found a stable home in the Lawrencetown Legion building by the early 1950s. It was at some point during that time, when Church became aware of Dr. Hall's educational trust. After much lobbying on Church's part, a brand new brick building was erected in 1958 on land donated by the Legion and served as the Nova Scotia Land Survey Institute until 1975. Now part of what constitutes the Nova Scotia Community College, Annapolis Valley campus, Lawrencetown is the "largest technical trainer of students in the geomatics field in Canada."

NORMAN D. PHINNEY (1912–1995)

The Phinneys trace their Valley roots to New England Planters Isaac Phinney and Zaccheus Phinney (a cousin or nephew of Isaac's) who settled at Granville between Bridgetown and Belleisle in the early 1760s. Zaccheus later moved to Paradise and raised his family while Isaac's son Lot established himself in Wilmot Township. The family is well represented today throughout Annapolis County in place names such as Phinney's Cove and Phinney's Brook along the Bay of Fundy, and sections of the North Mountain at Granville and Wilmot known as Phinney's Mountain.

From such pioneer stock came one of Nova Scotia's most respected and successful business families, best remembered perhaps for Phinney Music Co. Ltd. which for eighty years was a fixture on Barrington Street in Halifax. At the time of the photo (facing page, below right), Phinney's was said to be "one of Canada's leading music businesses and the most flourishing in the Maritimes." The store consisted of four levels. On the first were television and radio sets, electrical appliances, sheet music, and the "biggest collection of records in eastern Canada." Sporting goods, pianos, and organs were on the second floor with reconditioned pianos and offices on the third. The top level housed a service department. Unknown to most people is that the company has Valley roots, beginning at Lawrencetown, Annapolis County, in 1877 as a small organ store operated by Norman H. Phinney (1850-1919). Horton W. Phinney (1882-1966) joined his father's business, eventually transferring it to Halifax in 1912 and later opening stores in Wolfville, Kentville, Bridgewater, and New Glasgow. In 1918, Horton moved to Wolfville, living there seven years during which time he served as the town's mayor. In 1925, he returned to Halifax, establishing Maritime Finance Ltd., General Trust & Executor Corporation, and Scotian Gold Products Ltd. which in its time was one of the Valley's largest manufacturers of processed apples. During World War II, Horton and son Norman, who by then was heavily involved in the business side of things, purchased Kedgemakooge Lodge in Queens County. Originally established as a private rod and gun club for wealthy sportsmen in the early 1900s, it had fallen upon hard financial times because of the war. The Phinneys operated the property from 1944 to 1960 as a tourist business catering to summer families and autumn deer hunters, then sold it shortly before the land was expropriated and buildings torn down to make way for Kejimkujik National Park. Norman lived out his years at Wilmot, dedicating much time to helping establish the Annapolis Valley MacDonald Museum in nearby Middleton. The museum opened in 1982, and today houses a permanent display featuring Norman's extensive antique clock and watch collection.

BAND CONCERT, LAWRENCETOWN, 1926

Horton Phinney was an original member of the 69th Regimental Band when it organized at Lawrencetown in 1898. He became band director in 1908, conducting summer concerts at the bandstand as well as throughout surrounding communities. The white Studebaker was a taxi driven by Harold Ryan of Middleton who no doubt delivered a fare to the concert.

PHINNEY MUSIC CO. LTD., BARRINGTON STREET, HALIFAX, c.1948

An interesting snippet of radio trivia from the 1920s credits Horton Phinney with purchasing the first Marconi radio set made in Canada. Strange as it may seem today, Canadian law in the 1920s required every owner of a radio receiver such as the ones pictured to purchase a one-dollar license from the Minister of Transport. A label warning of dire consequence for non-compliance came attached to each set. In 1929, three hundred thousand licenses were issued; by 1937, the cost had risen to $2.50. Not until 1953 were licenses discontinued.

Commercial St. — Middleton, N. S.

MIDDLETON,
HEART OF THE
VALLEY.
THE TOWN'S
POPULATION IN
1891 WAS 740

Historians say Middleton "was born out of the serving of a transient public on its journeys through the length and breadth of this Valley." Early names— Gates Ferry, The Corners, Wilmot Corner, Fowlers Corner—are all indicative of its importance as a junction point for roads from both sides of the Annapolis River as well as those leading over the North Mountain to shipping ports on the Bay of Fundy. Even Middleton's present name and slogan, "Heart of the Valley," reflect its central geography. Regarding the formative years, W. A. Calnek writes:

> In 1834 there were two dwelling houses, possibly three, on the site of the handsome village now [1890] bearing the name of Middleton. Besides these there was a little store or shop in which the post-office was kept, and in which rum, tobacco and pipes, with a few other articles were kept for sale. One of these houses was used as an inn and there on Saturday after-noons, it was the custom of many of the farmers in the vicinity to meet for the purpose of gleaning the news of the past week and having a good social time. Liquor was freely indulged in, and sometimes, as usual every-where, to excess... At the beginning of the latter half of the century a manifest change became noticeable both in the people and the surround-ings of the corner. More thrift and greater temperance prevailed... Everybody began to look forward to the building up of a considerable town... In fact, taken altogether the rise of Middleton has been more rapid and more substantial than any other of our towns in the county.

The railway was a major factor in Middleton's turn around. Not only was it on the main line from Halifax to Yarmouth, but Middleton became an important terminus for south shore traffic in 1889 with the opening of the Nova Scotia Central Railway to Bridgewater. Only eighty-eight kilometres in length, the cross-province shortcut was very popular despite its snail-like speed. A steam locomotive leaving Middleton struggled one and a half hours to cover the first forty-five winding kilometres up and over the South Mountain to reach its first stop at Springfield. Nicknamed the Blueberry Express, legend claims a person could jump off the front of the train, pick a pail of berries and jump back on before it passed.

THE AMERICAN HOUSE, MIDDLETON, N. S.

AMERICAN HOUSE HOTEL, MIDDLETON Being a focal point for roads and railways, Middleton had a number of establishments catering to the traveller. There were four in the early 1900s—American House, Hatfield House, Spa Hotel (not to be confused with Spa Springs Hotel), and Middleton House. The American House was the last to go, closing in 1959, then torn down in 1966.

MIDDLETON'S ATHLETIC FIELD Baseball was played in Middleton as early as the 1890s. In 1905, this sports field was opened and in 1919 the Annapolis Valley Baseball League began with teams from Middleton, Kentville, Bridgetown, Annapolis Royal, and Digby. The large brick building to the right was the MacDonald Consolidated School which opened in 1904. The first consolidated school in the country, it was built with funds donated by tobacco manufacturer Sir William Christopher MacDonald, whom Queen Victoria called "the greatest philanthropist in education in the British Empire."

HAROLD RYAN (LEFT) AND HIS 1924 STUDEBAKER

Taxi driver Harold Ryan, left, and a questionable-looking individual, right, stand alongside Harold's 1924 eight passenger "Town Limousine" Studebaker which also doubled as a police car on occasion.

Middleton resident Harold Ryan drove the only taxi (one of the few in the Valley at the time) for seven years beginning in 1920 at the age of sixteen. He delivered fares to Halifax, Bridgewater, Digby, and pretty much everywhere in between, no mean feat considering the condition of the roads. Much of his business was derived from the trains that passed through Middleton at all hours of the day and night, but he also filled in as an ambulance and mail driver and any other job requiring the use of his car. Harold started with a 1919 Model T Ford but found it too small and lacking power and switched to Studebakers. Due to the nature of his work, Harold was granted a permit to carry a concealed weapon, a wise decision considering the following incident taken from his unpublished memoirs:

A couple of fur buyers from Montreal hired me to take them to Albany [Annapolis County], there being a trapper there who had some hides for sale. I left them and went back later. When getting near Middleton they asked me how much the trip would be and after I replied they said they had not decided if they would pay me or not. I replied they would pay me or they would not be leaving Middleton. Suddenly one of them grabbed me by the hair and tried to pull me over into the back seat. Instantly I pushed the brake pedal hard down which threw the two fur buyers forward almost into the front seat and the one let go his hold on my hair. I immediately pulled my Colt automatic from the holster and told them if they did not pay I would take them to the police chief. They paid the bill and I delivered them to the American House Hotel.

A. A. FORRESTALL

Albert Alawishis Forrestall was Middleton's long serving and only police constable. Forrestall also filled the duties of school janitor and town works caretaker and it was joked at the time of his retirement the town would have to hire three men to replace him. Because he had neither a car nor a gun, and Harold Ryan had both, Forrestall called upon him when the need arose.

One of those stories as told by Harold makes for interesting reading:

Prohibition days I well remember one particular incidence in which it seemed someone had bootleg liquor and a brawl was taking place. Mr. Forrestall called me about one o'clock in the morning and told me to be sure to take my automatic pistol. It so happened I carried the pistol with me at all times anyway. We were to search a place and try to find who had the liquor. After searching the house, Mr. Forrestall decided to look in the attic which meant going up through the trap door. He asked me to watch the ones involved while he searched. There were about twelve men and they acted very hostile so I stood in a corner with my hand in one pocket holding on to the good Colt automatic and I felt quite secure. We could not find any liquor but there was no more noise. Besides Mr. Forrestall I sometimes drove the county sheriff when necessary....

Lyshe, as Forrestall was commonly known, lived to be ninety-eight; he was the grandfather of Middleton native Tom Forrestall, the internationally acclaimed artist.

WILMOT SPA SPRINGS HOTEL

The health benefits of spas (abbreviation of Latin *salus per aquam* meaning "health from water") have been known since the dawn of ancient civilizations. The Valley had its own "Bluenose Fountain of Youth" in the late 1800s when throngs of people descended upon Middleton by train in an annual pilgrimage to the Wilmot Spa Mineral Springs just five kilometres from town on the road to Margaretsville. Patrons came from all parts of Atlantic Canada and points far beyond—Boston, New York, Philadelphia, Chicago, Los Angeles, even London, England. Their numbers included a who's who of the rich and famous, some of the more locally recognized celebrities being Samuel Cunard, Joseph Howe, Thomas Haliburton, Alexander Keith, and Prince George of Wales. Testimonials of miraculous healing powers flowed like the springs, some plausible, others crossing into the absurd, such as the claim (actually believed by some) that when an elderly soldier immersed his artificial corked leg in the waters, flesh began growing until it was completely covered!

The Wilmot Spa Springs odyssey began in 1817 when Farefield Woodbury, owner of the land upon which the three North Mountain springs are located, was advised by an unnamed gentleman well versed in the great spas of Britain, that Wilmot Springs had similar "healing virtues." When tested upon children with various maladies, they all recovered and so a legend was born. Woodbury built a few small bathhouses, piped in mineral water and fenced off the main spring. By the 1830s, Spa Springs had two large houses, which served as a hotel, filled to capacity, the overflow sleeping on floors of neighbouring farmhouses. In the 1880s, Captain Jacob Hall built a new three-storey Victorian-style Spa Springs Hotel for two hundred guests on the five acre pine grove, setting weekly rates at eight to twelve dollars, with discounts for longer stays. Many came not to board but simply drink from the springs—sometimes five pints in one sitting—while others sent casks to be filled. In 1889, Spa Springs Hotel burned to the ground and from then on, things went from bad to worse. The decision was made a year later to organize a consortium of Halifax and Kings County men into the Wilmot Spa Springs Company to market water under the brand name Spadeau (Spa Water); a factory was built on the site of the old hotel in 1891 to bottle soft drinks and aerated water. A new hotel (above) was erected but again destroyed by fire. The factory also burned in 1908, after which operations moved into Middleton for a time. The last bathhouse crumbled in the 1930s and to finish things, the pine grove was cut down during World War II to make lumber for constructing HMCS Cornwallis.

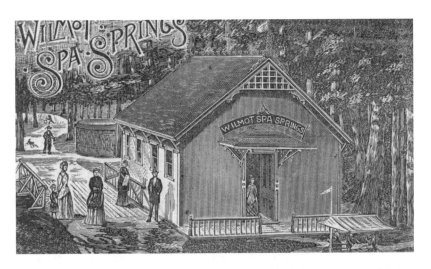

Historian Phyllis Blakeley writes that Spa Springs "had the reputation of being a gay place for those days, and puritanically inclined farmers objected to the breaking of the Sabbath." One mother was heard to tell her sons, "You go right to Sunday School, and don't let me hear of you hiding in the bushes watching those half-naked society husses play croquet." Extracurricular activities aside, the following excerpt from a brochure for Spadeau Natural Mineral Water touted it as a cure-all for just about whatever ailed a person:

> It has been shown that Spadeau is valuable as a medical agent. Strange, yet true, however freely it may be drank it does not create disorders, but exerts a prophylactic influence or prevents disease. It is a delicious, healthful beverage, it quenches thirst, prevents fermentations, aids digestion, and assists to assimilate the food. It agrees with the most delicate stomach, it cures indigestion and sick headaches. It is a most agreeable and cooling beverage to invalids...
>
> In point of fact, these waters have long been known as the most efficient in chronic gout and rheumatism, and the various disorders depending upon them. Dyspepsia—who that has experienced the sour or rancid eructations or regurgitations, flatulent distention and pain need any description of its unbearable melancholy horrors? Spadeau is an almost unfailing specific for this type of illness, when taken often during the day in small quantities. Spadeau is a mild laxative. Persons of a constipated habit may have most pleasant relief, and in many cases be permanently cured. It is a diuretic. Its salutary effect upon the kidneys is very marked. No doubt can exist respecting its efficiency in diseases of this class. In treatment of Urinary Concretions or Gravel, Spadeau has proven itself of great value... Great relief, and in many cases the permanent cure of most persistent Eczema, Tumors and Ulcers, from freely drinking Spadeau and applying it to the body in local application or by baths. Its value in these diseases is supposed to be due to the presence of Iodine, which it has been found to contain by recent analysis.
>
> It is rendered effervescent for table use by pure carbonic acid gas generated by the best methods known, and is fully equal to the most popular table water, and is put up in exactly the same way. It is with the utmost confidence, backed by the experience of half a century, that Spadeau is recommended as a table water which has no superior...

OLD HOLY TRINITY ANGLICAN CHURCH, MIDDLETON

In 1782, Reverend John Wiswall, a Loyalist from Boston, was sent to the Valley as a missionary, his parish covering an area of eight hundred square kilometres from Wolfville to Bridgetown. Six years later his duties were pared down considerably when the sprawling parish was divided and in 1789 Wiswall became the first Rector of the newly created Wilmot parish. Bishop Charles Inglis, who arrived at Halifax in 1787 having just been selected Nova Scotia's first bishop, left the squalor of the garrison town in 1789 and moved to the Valley where he built a home near Auburn, Kings County. He named his estate "Clermont" and lived there full time from 1796 to 1808 after which it served as a summer retreat until his death in 1816. Bishop Inglis instructed Wiswall to build a parish church at the far west end of Middleton in what today is known as the Pine Grove. With a grant of two hundred pounds from Governor John Parr, work began in 1789, and within two years the first service was held and the church consecrated. The building, however, remained unfinished until 1797, at which time the bell was installed. Old Holy Trinity served as the parish church until 1893, when a new Holy Trinity was built closer to the centre of Middleton. Abandoned for many years, Old Holy Trinity received a facelift in 2005 with the assistance of three levels of governmental funding on the occasion of its 214th anniversary. Now used for special occasions and still without electricity—the large windows of hand-blown glass providing the only light—Old Holy Trinity is claimed to be the only unaltered Loyalist church in Canada.

NICTAUX FALLS, 1890

A concrete dam 335 feet long and eight feet high was built here on the Nictaux River in 1911 to power an electric plant and concentrator for separating iron ore from rock.

The Nictaux River (from *Niktak* meaning "the forks of a river") tumbles down off the South Mountain to join up with the Annapolis River at Middleton. In 1789, Bishop Charles Inglis wrote in his journal, "We proceeded...to the Nictau [sic] settlement on the South Mountain. Here is a cataract of the River Nictau. Some men were busy erecting a furnace and forge to make iron. There is bog ore and upland ore in plenty but rather too distant from the furnace. I much doubt whether these men will succeed. The inhabitants of Nictau are about 156 families. They are from New England and removed here soon after the expulsion of the French neutrals about 1757." This is claimed to be the earliest record of smelting iron ore in Nova Scotia.

The Nictaux-Torbrook iron fields extend along the South Mountain from Middleton to Clementsport on the Annapolis Basin. It was at Clementsport in 1824-1826 where the first serious attempt was made to mine and smelt ore by the Annapolis Iron Mining Company but this "ill-directed effort" failed as did subsequent ventures between 1857 and 1885. The most ambitious undertakings to mine iron ore were centred at Nictaux and Torbrook in the years 1856 to 1913 under management of the Acadian Iron Mining Company from Londonderry, Colchester County. Mine shafts were sunk, smelting furnaces built, and spur rail lines laid to take ore out and bring Cape Breton coal in. As the focus switched from smelting to exporting, the seventy-five kilometre long Middleton & Victoria Beach Railway was built from Nictaux to Port Wade where ore was shipped to Pennsylvania, Scotland, and England. Eighty thousand dollars was spent to have a concentrator and electric plant installed at Nictaux for separating ore from rock, the waste then hauled to Middleton for building roads. Torbrook and Torbrook Mines were settlements that grew out of Nictaux, with each having its own post office by the 1890s. Employment was high with 125 men working underground in ten-hour shifts, six days a week, for $1.25 an hour; four were killed in mine accidents. Low production, however, could not keep up with world market demands, which led in part to closure of the mines in 1913. Little trace remains today. The generating plant continued to produce electricity until the mid-1950s when Nova Scotia Light & Power replaced it with a newer system. In addition to iron mining, several companies have worked granite quarries at Nictaux since 1889, with Heritage Memorials Ltd. still in operation.

Many thanks for your pretty card... I'm down there for a few weeks... Mr Mc Ma̶—ons store. Will write soon. — M. M. L.

Main Street, Kingston, N.S.

MAIN STREET, KINGSTON

Kingston's history can be confusing as there have been three communities in the general area with similar names—North Kingston (originally Rhodes), Kingston Village (now Greenwood Village) and present-day Kingston (known as Kingston Station until 1916), which sprung up when the railway came through in 1869. Main Street, Kingston (above) changed very little from this early-1900s rural image until an air force base was built at neighbouring Kingston Village during World War II.

The history of postcards is a story in itself that evolved over time. What at first glance appears to be random scribble on the face of the postcard seen here is in actuality the only area permitted by postal law for a salutatory message. The first Canadian postcards issued in 1871 were pre-stamped, plain cards used for business purposes which the post office sold for one cent, the price including delivery anywhere in the country. In 1898, private mailing cards like this one were introduced which reserved the stamped side of the card for address only. In 1903, a "divided back" postcard was issued which permitted address and message to appear on the same side of a card.

Delivering mail could be a grueling occupation. In 1909, Norman Grant, a farmer from Arlington, Annapolis County, signed a four-year contract to carry mail over the North Mountain to Bay of Fundy communities. He was paid an annual salary of $368, for which he agreed to travel by horse and wagon, or sleigh in winter, a total of 6,906 kilometres a year. Four days a week he started out at 7:30 A.M., keeping a mandatory average speed of eight kilometres an hour and ensuring no stop lasted more than seven minutes, the entire route to be completed within six hours. Grant was required to blow a "post horn" at regular intervals to alert people along the way so mails could be exchanged without loss of time.

DELIVERING THE RURAL MAIL

Photographer Clara Dennis snapped this picture of an unidentified mail driver on his delivery route near Kingston. The automobile parked off-road might indicate this was a chance encounter as Ms. Dennis (whose father William Dennis owned the Halifax Herald Newspaper Publishing Company) toured the province during the 1930s and 1940s snapping images of rural Nova Scotia.

COUNTRY POST OFFICES CAME IN ALL SHAPES AND SIZES

Mr. and Mrs. L. W. McLaughlin pose at entranceway to Wilmot Post Office, 1953. Mr. McLaughlin tended to postmaster duties while Mrs. McLaughlin delivered the mail. The McLaughlins originally built the quaint log structure during the war as a clubhouse for their sons and friends. It remains standing today off Highway 1 in Wilmot although the roofline has seen better days.

MAIN GATE TO ROYAL AIR FORCE BASE GREENWOOD, 1942

The British Commonwealth Air Training Plan is considered to have been Canada's most significant military contribution during World War II. The massive undertaking cost $2.2 billion and involved building more than one hundred air fields across the country. By war's end, 130,000 air crew members including pilots, wireless operators, air gunners, and navigators had been trained for the air forces of Great Britain, Australia, New Zealand, and Canada. In the fall of 1939, preliminary aerial surveys were flown over the Valley to identify possible sites for one of the air fields. This was followed up in 1940 by ground surveyors who concentrated their work in the area between Middleton and present-day Greenwood (which at the time comprised the two communities of Greenwood Square and Kingston Village). Nictaux was originally considered but ruled out because of its close proximity to the South Mountain. The decision was made to build sixteen kilometres to the east at Greenwood where fifteen parcels of land totalling 670 acres were initially purchased, with more acquired later for housing. Bulldozers began clearing land in late 1941 and by March 1942 the base was ready to be occupied, albeit in a rustic state. Four hundred airmen and twenty-eight officers arrived at Halifax that month from England aboard the *Athena*, then took a troop train to Kingston where they disembarked for the five-kilometre march to the base, many thinking they were in Kingston, Ontario. Facilities and comforts at Greenwood were spartan at the outset; however, life was made considerably easier by Kingston and Middleton residents who welcomed them with social and recreational activities. On average, training courses at Greenwood lasted three months with fifteen crews at a time receiving lecture, ground, and aerial instruction. Anson and Hudson were the first aircraft used, with airmen flying low level sub detection runs over the Bay of Fundy. In 1944, the Royal Canadian Air Force assumed command of Greenwood from the Royal Air Force. Much has transpired since then, but more than sixty years later Greenwood remains a key component of Canada's maritime military defence and a mainstay of the Valley's economy. The combined population in 1900 of Greenwood, Kingston, North Kingston, and Middleton was 2,622; the 2001 census put it at 7,054.

Camp Aldershot, Aylesford Plain, Kings County, 1898

Militia hold a storied place in the Valley's history going back to at least 1758 when an act was passed stating that "all male persons, planters, and inhabitants, and their servants, between the ages of sixteen and sixty, residing in and belonging to this province shall bear arms and duly attend all musters and military exercises." Eaton writes that "immediately after the New England Planters came to Nova Scotia, in every township where they settled militia regiments were formed, the officers receiving their commissions from the government at Halifax." Early militia units were poorly armed and trained but they served a purpose. During the Napoleonic Wars, a company from Annapolis marched 216 kilometres to Halifax in thirty-five hours, served four weeks bolstering the garrison town's defences, then marched home. Militia were called upon in the War of 1812 to fend off American privateers raiding coastal communities and again in 1866 to man the borders against the Fenian threat. Following Confederation in 1867, when militia became a federal government responsibility, Canada was divided into nine military districts, one being Nova Scotia. The province was subsequently broken down into nineteen regimental divisions, three of which consisted of Kings, Annapolis, and Digby counties, each comprised of smaller community regiments. At some point, believed to have been 1880 or possibly earlier, the "sandy Aylesford plain, near the Annapolis County line" in the vicinity of Auburn (above) was designated a summer and fall militia training ground. Units from throughout Nova Scotia came to Camp Aldershot (named after the famed army facility in the south of England), but the cramped grounds, wedged between the D. A. R. tracks and Highway 1, restricted military manouevres. The tent camp became more noted for its bouts of fisticuffs and disease than battlefield drill, a deficiency magnified by Canadian losses incurred in the Boer War of 1899-1901. Sir Frederick Borden, federal Minister of Militia and a native of Canning, Kings County, lost a son in the conflict who had trained at Aldershot. At Borden's persistent urging, the Dominion government allotted twenty-five thousand dollars in 1903 to purchase 2,500 acres north of Kentville to establish a new Camp Aldershot where thousands of army personnel trained during both world wars. Today Aldershot serves as a militia (army reserve) training base.

KELLY VILLA, AYLESFORD

Kelly Villa was built in 1906 by William J. Kelly from Brooklyn, New York, as a summer retreat for his wife Lizetta, whose father William Sandford was a merchant and hotel keeper at Harbourville. The wealthy Kelly, who made his money in the printing business, hired noted Aylesford architect L. R. Fairn to design and oversee building the "palatial residence." At Fairn's insistence, only local labour was used. The expansive property of 170 acres was located five kilometres from Aylesford on the side of the North Mountain, providing a commanding view of the Valley. To make the house fit its surroundings, Fairn had to first cut away parts of the mountain and fill in others. A long driveway paved with beach stone from the Bay of Fundy led to the grand twenty-one room Kelly Villa that included a three-storey circular tower, observation balcony, and piazza along two sides. Built from the finest native and imported woods at a cost of fifteen thousand dollars, a princely sum for the times, the modified mission-style mansion was equipped with all the conveniences including the newest Natura toilet seat and Kenny flushmeter. What had Valley tongues wagging, however, was its electrical plant. A ten-horsepower gasoline engine from Lloyd's in Kentville, fed from seven underground fuel barrels, ran a dynamo that powered eighty lights (of sixteen to thirty-two candle power), a water pump, and numerous electrical outlets into which were plugged ventilating fans, curling tongs, room heaters, irons, cooking utensils, and even cigar lighters. On summer evenings, the North Mountain was "all aglitter [with] dazzling light" that could be seen from miles around. For twenty-two years, Kelly Villa dominated the landscape. In August 1928, however, Lizetta (then Mrs. Sandford Kelly Hallet and recently widowed for the second time), put the estate up for sale at ten thousand dollars, an advertisement claiming the "buildings alone worth twice the price asked." In November, the house with all its contents mysteriously burned to the ground, a willful act attributed to an arsonist who had been terrorizing Aylesford for months. With Kelly Villa in ashes, and Lizetta having moved to the U.S., the barn was used as a community dance hall until the late 1930s when it was destroyed by lightning.

CAMP AT LOON LAKE, KINGS COUNTY, 1887

Boiling a kettle at Loon Lake near Aylesford Lake, Kings County, 1887. (Left to right: Will Skinner, Wall Skinner, Bill Kreekele).

With Nova Scotia widely renowned as a hunting and fishing mecca for non-resident sportsmen in the early 1900s, there were many spots along the Dominion Atlantic Railway through the Valley where "sports" could procure lodgings and hire the services of local guides. Hotels offered daily rates of $1.50 to $2.00 with discounts by the week; guides charged $2.00 to $3.00 a day, possibly $5.00 if a camp and meals were needed. A wide choice of sporting grounds within access of wagon and team were to be found on the South Mountain side of the Valley. Torbrook, Albany, Albany Cross, New Albany, Nictaux, Dalhousie, Dalhousie West, Long Lake, Four Mile Lake, Lake Alma, Lake George, and Lake Paul were all endorsed in tourist booklets as having "wooded and barren lands, bogs, rivers and lakes where all kinds of game find a home." The above image is from a photo album collection of sporting activities and touring shots taken of Kings County in the late 1880s by an American photographer visiting with friends near South Berwick. A brief handwritten note accompanied the album: "Reminders of pleasant times in 1887-88. From your friend Rens Spaans." A postscript mentions the party caught 1,200 trout during that summer visit.

WEST KINGS MEMORIAL HOSPITAL

Postcard of West Kings Memorial Hospital at Berwick, showing 1951 addition in the foreground. Architect Leslie R. Fairn designed the original hospital, which cost $35,000 to build.

The Nova Scotia Legislature passed an act on February 15, 1896, granting financial assistance to any community willing to establish a hospital. The Local Hospital Act provided annual funding of fifteen cents per day per patient up to a maximum of five hundred dollars per hospital, dependent upon regular governmental inspections. The earliest medical facilities, of which the Valley had several, were small scale, generally housed in semi-converted private dwellings, giving rise to the term "cottage hospitals." Severe medical cases still had to be sent by train to the Victoria General Hospital (established in 1859) in Halifax. With the return of thousands of injured and disabled soldiers from the Great War in 1918, there began a concerted effort on the part of many communities to build proper hospitals as memorials to Canadian veterans. The first publicly funded hospital between Windsor and Yarmouth officially opened in Berwick on June 3, 1922, the date picked to coincide with a national holiday marking the birthday of King George V. Built largely from money raised through community bazaars and donations, the initial cost for a stay in one of the sixteen ward beds at West Kings Memorial Hospital was two dollars a day. In the first year of operation, thirty-one of the hospital's 120 patients were from Berwick, the rest from Kings County. Operational expenses in 1923 were covered by grants from Kings County, the town of Berwick, and the provincial "allowance," which by then had risen to thirty cents per day per patient for the first five thousand patient days, twenty cents per day thereafter. Total expenditures for the first year were less than five thousand dollars, the small amount perhaps attributable to a flock of "hospital hens" that were kept to eat scraps and supply eggs. A letter from Mayor Samuel Chipman Parker in the *Berwick Register*, December 30, 1925 stated, "Kings Memorial Hospital has had a busy year, never more so than during the holiday season. About fifteen patients are being cared for there, and service seems to be the watchword of the Hospital staff... The importance of the Hospital as a financial asset to the community...does a larger business than the Town of Berwick. The total receipts for the last financial year were $10,833.18 and expenditures on maintenance were $9,199.94 with an additional $1,500 paid on capital account." A brick wing was added in 1951, increasing the number of beds to twenty-eight but driving the daily expense up to six dollars. On November 14, 1967, a brand-new hospital with seventy-four beds opened, the cost then skyrocketing to $29.50 per diem.

Peat is comprised of the "partially decomposed remains of plants and animals which have accumulated in oxygen poor, water saturated, freshwater environments." Through the course of world history, peat moss has served many purposes—eighteenth-century building blocks for paupers' homes, a horticultural growing medium, a filter for gases, odours, and liquids, and fuel to generate electricity. When mixed with tar and plaster of Paris, peat moss has been moulded into insulating materials and wadding. The ice age of eleven thousand years ago left behind numerous peat bogs throughout Nova Scotia that have been forming at the rate of thirty centimetres per thousand years. More than one-half of the four hundred thousand acres of peat land are found in the southwestern counties of Yarmouth, Queens, and Shelburne. Once considered little more than wastelands, a peat moss industry began developing after World War II in Quebec, New Brunswick, Nova Scotia, and Maine. The only company presently mining peat moss in Nova Scotia is the Annapolis Valley Peat Moss Company Ltd., established in 1949 at Berwick (with three affiliate companies now operating in Prince Edward Island). Berwick was a natural choice with the expansive Caribou Bog just to the west of town. Various sites from Kentville to Kingston have been mined over the years, some now drained and used for growing vegetables. Current annual peat moss production for Nova Scotia is estimated at two hundred thousand bales, with export markets including the United States, Japan, England, Holland, Germany, and Saudi Arabia. It is said that Annapolis Valley Peat Moss Company Ltd. has a remaining peat deposit of ten million bales available from 740 acres in Nova Scotia. Before peat moss, cranberries were harvested from the Caribou Bog. In 1892, Spurgeon Bishop of Auburn shipped the first railcar load of cranberries from Kings County and by 1908, the village of Aylesford was exporting five thousand barrels a year.

BERWICK, THE "CAMP MEETING TOWN," 1908

In the early 1800s, Methodism had placed the Valley "under a deep religious influence." At the crossroads of Black Rock Road and Brooklyn Street, Kings County, for example, the corner was named Grafton around 1847 for a church that was cut in two at the centre, then rejoined after a section was added to accommodate revival meetings. Although the landmark building was demolished more than thirty years ago, an enduring testament to John Wesley's doctrine remains today at Berwick. Featured on these pages are three 1908 postcard images of the Methodist Camp Meeting Grounds. The idea for a camp was born in 1871, when Edward C. Foster, a native of Bridgetown then living in Berwick, attended a Methodist camp while conducting business in Boston. Upon his return, Foster convinced local church elders of the need for something similar here. In 1872, on a hemlock wooded twenty-three acre lot in Berwick, Methodist congregations from throughout Nova Scotia gathered to begin erecting prayer meeting "society tents" based upon directives outlined in the official *Camp Meeting Manual* from the United States. Accommodations were also made to feed the anticipated masses and shelter horses. The first camp meeting was held on Friday, July 5, 1872, and continued until the following Thursday. Extra trains were needed to bring in the throngs of worshippers, which on Sunday swelled to three thousand people, triple Berwick's population at the time. Three services were held daily with eighteen preachers delivering sermons. The inaugural camp meeting was such a resounding success that plans were immediately made to have it become an annual event. Over the years, Sunday crowds (largest of the week) drew more than five thousand worshippers, some from as far away as New York, Boston, and Saint John, New Brunswick. Tents eventually gave way to a variety of buildings including more than seventy cottages. As a result of Church Union in 1925, the camp meeting grounds became the property of the United Church of Canada which still operates it through the Camp Meeting Association. Going strong after 134 years, today's Berwick Camp, while still offering its trademark ten-day "encampments," has evolved into a multi-use, multi-denominational Christian family camp.

COTTAGES AT METHODIST CAMP MEETING GROUNDS, BERWICK

ENTRANCE TO CAMP GROUNDS, BERWICK A message written on the back of one postcard read: "We got here all right, feel tired. Swept the cob webs down; tidied up and got our tea at the dining hall. I wish you were here too, they are singing at the pavilion. Hope you are all well. Lovingly, Mother."

KENTVILLE TRAIN STATION (1869–1990)

Kentville today is the Valley's largest municipality with a population of 5,610. The town was originally called Horton Corner by the Planters, a name changed in 1826 to honour Prince Edward, Duke of Kent, who stopped over in 1794 when commander of British military forces in the province. Kentville was little more than a hamlet until the coming of the railway in 1869, when its population nearly tripled within two years. For more than a century after, the Shiretown of Kings County was railway central, first for the Windsor and Annapolis line, then the Dominion Atlantic Railway. Much is written of the main route through the Valley but there was another line of only twenty kilometres (thirteen miles) from Kentville to Kingsport known as the Cornwallis Valley Railway that also deserves mention. Opened in 1890 to carry freight, mail, and passengers back and forth, the railway proved its worth in the first year, ferrying twenty thousand passengers and ten thousand tons of freight. A branch line, North Mountain Railway, was added in 1914 between Centreville and Weston to accommodate farmers who needed a more efficient means of moving copious quantities of apples and potatoes to markets in Halifax. By the early 1930s the Cornwallis Valley Railway was making two round trips a day along both lines, sometimes three on Saturdays. The trains were affectionately known as "Blueberry Specials" for the low-growth bushes which lined the tracks. Off-duty railway workers frequently used their passes to ride the train, jump off at some point going out, leisurely fill a pail or two, and be ready for pick up on the return trip. With roads in poor condition much of the year, people came to depend upon the C. V. R. as their principal means of travel to shop and work. For eighty-five cents, a person could purchase a return ticket and take in a Saturday movie in Kentville. Five days a week, high school students from Kingsport, Canning, and Sheffield Mills rode the train to and from Kentville Academy; class times were set to train schedules with a three month travel pass costing three dollars and thirty cents. The last Blueberry Special made a run in 1961, although it would be 1993 before the Cornwallis Valley Railway's remaining piece of track between Kentville and Steam Mill Village was officially abandoned. The berry bushes, too, disappeared from track side with no rail workers to burn them every two years to encourage regeneration, as was customary. The North Mountain Railway branch operated until 1962.

**CORNWALLIS INN,
KENTVILLE, 1950S**

The Cornwallis Inn at Kentville was one of the three luxury hotels the Canadian Pacific Railway owned along the Land of Evangeline line from Yarmouth to Halifax. In 1919, the C. P. R. purchased the three-storey Aberdeen Hotel built near the Kentville train station in 1892 by Daniel McLeod. Renamed the Cornwallis Inn, it was used until this new hotel opened in 1930 on Main Street. Built in just 208 days, it had all the class and amenities of its sister hotels in Digby and Yarmouth including ninety guest rooms, four luxury suites, ten "sample rooms" for travelling salesmen, dining room, lounge, ballroom, and meeting rooms. In 1963, perhaps as a harbinger of things to come, the hotel underwent extensive renovations. The steps, verandas, gardens, walkways, and ivy featured in this photo were all removed and a shopping arcade added with half of the guest rooms converted to apartments. Ten years later the hotel closed and in 1976 it was totally converted to apartments and businesses. Lakeside Inn at Yarmouth shut its doors in 1960, after which it became a nursing home—St. Joseph's Villa Du Lac. Only the Pines Hotel in Digby remains operational today under ownership of the provincial government.

ORIGINAL WHITE SPOT CANTEEN, NEW MINAS, 1947

POSTCARD OF WHITE SPOT RESTAURANT & MOTEL, C.1980

The village of New Minas, located between Kentville and Wolfville, has experienced phenomenal retail growth in recent years lending it the moniker "Shopping Centre of the Valley." It is a deserving title attested to by anyone familiar with the traffic congestion along the narrow roadway bisecting its numerous strip malls, box stores, and specialty shops. Many remember a far different New Minas when a long-time fixture of the once pastoral community was the White Spot Restaurant & Motel, a well-patronized rest stop for travelling salesmen. The White Spot began in 1946 when Charles and Midge Simons opened a roadside canteen (above) in front of their farmhouse on Highway 1. Equipment was minimal with only a hot plate and a couple of stools; George and Myrtle Perrier were their first customers. William Milligan purchased the White Spot in 1951; two years later it burned to the ground but was immediately replaced with a small restaurant that was enlarged several times to eventually seat 106 customers. A twelve-unit motel was added in 1956, which by 1969 had been enlarged to forty-six rooms. William Milligan, Jr. took over the business in 1992 but unfortunately, the era of the travelling salesman had passed the White Spot by. In 1993 the landmark was razed and an Atlantic Superstore was built on the site.

POSTCARD DRAW-
ING OF ACADIA
UNIVERSITY, 1920.
AN ACCOMPANYING
CAPTION READ:
"PHOTO OF A CHAR-
COAL DRAWING BY
AN AMERICAN ART-
IST. DRAWN 1920
AND PICTURES
FUTURE DIAGRAM
OF ACADIA
GROUNDS."

In 1829, Baptists opened Horton Academy, from which Acadia College was born ten years later. Considered one of Canada's premiere undergraduate universities today, it could be said that Acadia has kept Wolfville forever young. From an initial student body in double digits, enrollment has grown to where Wolfville's population of approximately thirty-six hundred residents temporarily swells to more than seven thousand each September. Arguably two communities working as one, many from the legions of Acadia alumni never leave the Valley, while the majority who do invariably take a part with them.

Tom Sheppard writes in his comprehensive *Historic Wolfville* that "Wolfville was chosen as a site [for Acadia] because of its natural beauty and its central position." The same applies more than 175 years later. Widely touted as the "academic and cultural hub" of the Valley today, a Government of Canada 2004 Labour Market Review also places Wolfville within what socio-economic studies term the "Kentville-New Minas-Wolfville Corridor," one of the fastest-growing residential and trade "urban corridors" in Nova Scotia. The population of Kings County in 1891 was 22,489; in 2001 it stood at 58,866. In realtor language, location is everything and so it is with the "corridor," where forty percent of Kings County residents now live. Just as the railway opened up the eastern Valley in the 1870s, so too did the provincial highway in the 1970s. Now only a one-hour drive from Halifax (and soon to be even more accessible with the ever-approaching twinned highway), eastern Kings County has become popular with those seeking the rural life but who also, by choice or necessity, desire to remain within commuting distance of the provincial capital. Not surprisingly, since 1987, the region has exceeded the average provincial employment rates. With the Valley's geographical restraints and agricultural tradition, farmers and developers must compromise, as the trend to this point has been "town surrounds" with highest population growth on the periphery of established municipalities.

The following three Nova Scotia Information Service photos taken in the 1950s, while obviously staged for tourism purposes, capture some of the diverse beauty that attracts people to eastern Kings County (see next two pages). Looking down upon the Valley from Blomidon, it is readily apparent why the Mi'kmaq god Glooscap, (*Gloos* meaning "good," as in friend), made the North Mountain home. A 1924 Nova Scotia travelogue claimed that from here "six rivers [can be] seen wending their way to the great Basin; as many towns are in plain view, and the eye is able to distinguish points of interest in at least five different counties."

GASPEREAU VALLEY

The Gaspereau Valley can best be described as a valley within the Valley, part of but separated from it by the glacially formed "Wolfville Ridge." The area attracted both Mi'kmaq and Acadians because of the river's bountiful stocks of salmon, smelt, and gaspereau. Once an apple and lumber producing region, the Gaspereau today is known for its grapes; it is one of five locations in the Valley with vineyards and a winery.

LOW TIDE AT MINAS BASIN

The Minas Basin, in geological jargon, is a "silted-up remnant of a 200 million-year old rift valley once located near the equator." Twice daily when the tides have retreated five kilometres seaward, nearly one hundred thousand acres of sand and mud (more than one-third of the entire basin area) lies exposed. The Bay of Fundy and its sub-basins are a naturalist's smorgasbord, serving up sandstone formations, fossils, minerals, wildlife and waterfowl, salt marshes, zooplankton, fish, and subterranean life.

HANTSPORT
WATERFRONT,
C.1950.
PROMINENT
BUILDINGS:
FAR RIGHT, FUNDY
GYPSUM CO. LTD;
CENTRE, MINAS
BASIN PULP &
POWER CO. LTD.;
FAR LEFT,
CANADIAN KEYES
FIBRE CO. LTD.,
THE FORMER SITE
OF THE CHURCHILL
SHIPYARD

The town of Hantsport (current population 1,250) sits just inside Hants County on the Avon River. Until 1849, it was known as Halfway River for being at the mid-point between Windsor and Grand Pré. Hantsport's legacy is shipbuilding, thanks in large measure to Ezra Churchill, who moved from Yarmouth in the late 1830s to establish one of the province's most famous and productive shipyards, a business his sons John and George carried on until the 1890s. Hantsport's economic fortunes took a decided downturn when the days of wooden ships and iron men passed into history, a downward spiral that continued until the early 1900s. Unlike other communities that never regained their feet, Hantsport rebounded thanks to one man who, when he passed away in 1973 at the age of eighty-four, left behind the wealthiest family empire in Nova Scotia today. Roy Jodrey, whose father Joe moved to Hantsport in the late 1800s from Lunenburg, left school at the age of twelve, having already started two businesses. By 1957, he reportedly held more directorships, fifty-six, than any other Canadian. What Jodrey lacked in education was more than made up for by "sheer determination and street smarts." When demand for electricity grew, he (and Charles Wright from Wolfville) built a dam and generating plant at White Rock on the Gaspereau River in 1919 and sold power to the Valley. When industry in Nova Scotia moved from lumber to pulp and paper, Jodrey built the Minas Basin Pulp & Power Company Ltd. in 1927 at Hantsport (top centre); six years later he opened the Canadian Keyes Fibre plant (left) to make fibre products such as egg cartons, paper plates, and food containers. Both businesses are still going strong today. Roy Jodrey has been described as being from the old school, "a man whose word was as good as his bond." Biographer Harry Bruce writes, "His place was the Valley…he was [a] pre-eminent home-grown industrialist…the Valley boy who not merely made a million but who stayed right here in the Valley."

Nova Scotia is one of the most productive gypsum-mining regions in the world. Fundy Gypsum Co. Ltd. (top right), a subsidiary of U. S. Gypsum, started out at Windsor in 1924, then moved its shipping facilities to Hantsport in 1946. One of the fastest loading ports in North America, a freighter can dock on the rising tide and be ready to sail in less than three hours at high tide with forty thousand tons of raw gypsum.

STOCKPILING GYPSUM

Hants County sits on a bed of gypsum which has been quarried since the Acadians farmed the area. Farmers made extra cash mining small quantities found on their lands, then hauling it to one of several ports in the Windsor-Hantsport area for sale to shippers. Narrow gauge rail lines like these were often used in larger quarry operations which provided much-needed employment.

LOADING GYPSUM

Shipments out of the Windsor and Hantsport area generally went first to Saint John and St. Andrews, New Brunswick, then on to the United States, which has historically taken ninety percent or more of production. Gypsum was known as "land plaster" until 1900 because it was used primarily as fertilizer (and a filler in paints). During the early twentieth century, demand grew for its importance in manufacturing plaster of Paris and to retard the cement-setting process. Production took off in the mid-1900s with the invention of gyprock.

GERRISH STREET, WINDSOR, C.1935

The Great Fire of 1897 burned eighty percent of Windsor—five hundred buildings—making it the worst town disaster in Nova Scotia's history. Windsor is known as the "Little Town of Big Firsts," the site of the first college in Canada (King's College School, 1788); the first library in Canada (1790); the birthplace of hockey (an ongoing debate with the rest of Canada); the first Bank of Nova Scotia branch (1837); the first public railway in Nova Scotia (1858); the first town in Canada with a covered rink (1870); and the first telephones in Nova Scotia (1872). Windsor is also the birthplace of Canadian icon Thomas Chandler Haliburton (1796-1865), "lawyer, judge, politician, writer and Father of American Humour." A more recent celebrity of international fame is farmer Howard Dill, progenitor of the world's largest pumpkins.

WAITING FOR THE TIDE, WINDSOR, 1950S

During the period 1836 to 1890, Windsor was Canada's third-largest port behind Montreal and Saint John; in 1840, 525 vessels called. Gypsum, lumber, and pulpwood were primary exports until the mid-1900s; of the 100,424 tons of gypsum shipped out of Hants County in 1869 to the U.S., 81,276 tons passed through Windsor. Building a causeway across the Avon River in 1970 sealed any possibility, however remote, of Windsor ever returning to its shipping days.

Chapter 4

Over to the Shore

FUNDY'S RUGGED BEAUTY

There are more than twenty hamlets along the Fundy coast between Delaps Cove and Halls Harbour. Isolated from the Valley by the North Mountain but an integral part of its history, they make up what is known as the Bay Shore. Fishing, farming, and trade were once their lifeblood. It took a special breed of person to eke out an existence here in the early years amid the cliffs and turbulent waters. One need only drive the Ox Bow, a switchback section of Route 360 leading from Berwick to Harbourville, for an appreciation of the daunting task once faced to crest the mountain burdened with heavy loads. Those days are long gone. What hasn't changed is the rugged coastal beauty and a determined spirit among those who live here to keep alive what remains of their communities.

DELAPS COVE, 1950S

Calnek writes in his history of Annapolis County, "It was about [1799] that roads to the Bay of Fundy began to be felt necessary…Those to Parker's Cove, to Young's Cove, to Chute's Cove, to Delaps Cove to Phinney's Cove and others were rapidly opened and settlements formed…. The names of these coves were those of the owners of the lots whose homes were by the [Annapolis] river side…The northern shores became dotted with the cottages of the farmer and the fisherman, especially in the neighbourhood of the coves, and roads were soon afterwards made from cove to cove along the shores, thus affording fresh facilities for new settlements." In 1891, Annapolis County's population was 19,350; today it is 21,773 with nearly twenty percent, four thousand people, still living along the Bay Shore.

During the early- to mid-1800s much of the product and produce from the Valley destined for export was shipped from Bay Shore ports. The *Yarmouth Herald* of August 18, 1837, carried the following:

> In a period of nineteen days in 1837, coasting vessels "almost wholly from the shores of the Bay of Fundy [carried] to the city of Saint John, New Brunswick: 733,500 feet deals; 1,192 tons plaister [sic]; 4,323 dozen eggs; 2,260 boxes smoked herrings; 98 barrels pickled herrings; 187 boxes cherries; 4,074 lbs. butter; 5,902 lbs. cheese; 603 bushels potatoes; 236,000 staves; 55,000 shingles; 10 horses; 951 sheep and lambs; 16 oxen; 5 cows; 25 calves; 1,000 gallons oil; 88,000 feet boards; 67 flagging stones; 1 barrel shad; 2 barrels codfish; 60 bushels oats; 4 barrels and 58 bottles fir balsam; 34,000 bricks; 1520 quintals dry fish; 1 qtl. scaled fish; 900 lbs. hops; 55 sides leather; 20 empty barrels; 28 cords wood; 7 barrels tongues and sounds; 2 barrels pork; 24 chairs; 840 lbs. ham; 7,000 feet lumber; 456 lbs. smoked meat; 22,000 feet scantling; 27,800 feet hardwood boards and lumber. On a rough calculation we conclude that the value of these articles is about 7500 pounds [$18,000.]. Export business has been this brisk every month for years past.

PARKER'S COVE, EARLY 1900S

PORT GEORGE, 1895

Building the railway in the late 1800s adversely affected Bay Shore communities more than those in the Valley. Parker's Cove, not being a shipping port, survived the transition fairly well, continuing to build small fishing vessels and fish scallops. In 1891, its population was 569; by the mid-1950s, it had been more than halved to 225. Port George was devastated by its loss of Valley trade to Saint John and Boston; a population numbering 684 in 1891, had shrunk to just eighty-four by 1956. Today, only a handful of buildings and the lighthouse (which now sits on land because the wharves are gone) remain from the prosperous scene pictured here. Two other communities situated between Parker's Cove and Port George saw their numbers reduced by more than half from 1891 to 1956: Hampton from 374 to 171 and Port Lorne from 673 to 222.

MARGARETSVILLE
LIGHTHOUSE, ONE
OF SEVERAL
ALONG THE BAY
SHORE, WAS
BUILT IN 1859

Owing to Nova Scotia's maritime geography, there is much truth to a time-worn saying that if you don't like the weather, wait five minutes. Just ask anyone in the Valley when unexpected winter snow squalls blow in over the North Mountain. Nearly surrounded as the province is by the Bay of Fundy, Atlantic Ocean, and Gulf of St. Lawrence, and in the northerly path of the Gulf Stream, the sometimes questionable accuracy of meteorological forecasts have always been a popular subject of conversation. One constant, however, is that with the relative coolness of summertime ocean temperatures and their relative warmth in winter, coastal areas of Nova Scotia experience moderate temperatures. Studies show the Valley benefits most, averaging 140 frost-free days per year (ideal for farmers) and enjoying the warmest temperatures in Nova Scotia. The North and South Mountains are responsible for this, but at the same time they block onshore breezes during the dog days of summer, which can result in stifling temperatures. Then is the time that Valley residents have traditionally headed "over to the shore" for a respite. People came to Margaretsville from far and wide. There was a time, still within memory, when Sunday was an accepted day of rest, and an afternoon family drive was as much a part of devotionals as morning church attendance. Patrons of Spa Springs frequented Margaretsville as did airmen from Greenwood during World War II. There are even stories of German submariners enjoying a bit of clandestine shore leave at weekend dances. Margaretsville could even boast of a haunted lighthouse to add to its allure. Legend says that one keeper of the light would doff his hat upon entering the building, bow and say, "Good Evening, Dave." This was to acknowledge the resident spirit, claimed to be that of a man who committed suicide by jumping from the wharf at high tide. His body was later recovered and left to lie overnight in the lighthouse before being whisked away to the cemetery the following day and buried in an unmarked grave.

THE TEA ROOM IN MARGARETSVILLE

Margaretsville was popular with its tea room and five-cent-a-scoop, home-made ice cream topped off by a "salubrious and delightfully cool atmosphere." Note the throngs of people on the wharf queuing for a boat ride. Originally a shipping port with a population of 703 in 1891, the village turned to fishing and tourism after the railway was built. By 1956, there were 311 people living in the village, which had two hotels and numerous summer homes.

MARGARETSVILLE

MORDEN, KINGS COUNTY, 1890S

In 1783, James Morden, an Ordnance Yard storekeeper in Halifax who had fought with Wolfe at Quebec, was granted five thousand acres in Aylesford Township where he built a summer residence near what is now Auburn. Included in his lands, which stretched to the Bay of Fundy, was French Cross, which then consisted of only a few fishermen's huts. In 1790, Morden donated six acres of land at Auburn and paid one-third of the construction costs to have St. Mary's Anglican Church built on condition he and his heirs be given pew number eight in perpetuity. Soldiers carried doors, windows, and nails 140 kilometres from Halifax. Ironically, some of the plaster for the church was made from burning quahog shells to make lime—shells the Acadians had left at French Cross during the winter of 1755 when many died attempting to escape the English deportation. St. Mary's is one of the earliest consecrated Anglican churches in British North America; Edward, Duke of Kent worshiped there in 1797, then visited Bishop Inglis's Clermont estate. Following Morden's death in 1792, nothing noteworthy appears concerning the grant until 1833, when it reverted to Colonel John Butler, Commissary General living in London. Between 1835 and 1868, Butler transformed the tiny hillside fishing hamlet into "a considerable village," laying it out along three parallel running streets in typical military fashion and changing the name from French Cross to Morden.

ANGLICAN CHRIST CHURCH, MORDEN, 1890S

Colonel Butler had Christ Church built in 1854; it burned in 1905 but was rebuilt within five years. Morden became well known throughout the Valley in the early 1900s for its summer tea meetings put on by ladies of the community's three churches—Anglican, Methodist, and Roman Catholic. People came by land and sea to attend the all-day fundraisers that included copious quantities of cooked and baked food carried in trunks from parish homes by horse and wagon. Bands played, canteens sold confectioneries, and scrubbed-down fishing boats provided cruises for ten cents. An evening square dance traditionally closed out the gala event.

MORDEN'S ONE-ROOM SCHOOL

Church and school were the pillars of every community. Historian Arthur Eaton writes in his Kings County history that prior to the Free School Act of 1865 a contract "was made directly between the 'Proprietors' of the school, as the parents were called, and the teacher.... The teacher pledged himself to give instruction in reading, writing and arithmetic. Sometimes he added the extra branches of grammar and geography. The patrons bound themselves to provide schoolroom, fuel, and board for the teacher. The further item of salary was variously designated ... For many years the teacher 'boarded round', that is, lived house to house, his sojourn varying from three or four days to as many weeks, according to the number of pupils that the various homes sent him."

MORDEN WHARF, 1890s

W. A. Calnek wrote in his *History of the County of Annapolis*: "The Bay of Fundy coast affords no natural harbours...though artificial breakwaters have been constructed which do duty in their stead, by the aid of which a large trade is carried on..." Morden's first breakwater was built around 1842.

FISHING WEIR (FAR RIGHT) AT MORDEN

In 1891, there were twenty-two businesses curing fish in Annapolis County. Calnek reported that "among the industries...must be reckoned the herring fisheries...Weirs are annually put up on the sand-bars and flats...and the cost of outlay and construction is very frequently rewarded by valuable catches." According to Eaton, "From the earliest settlement of the county [Kings], fishing has been carried on in Minas Basin and the rivers and along the Bay Shore... In 1861 there were engaged in fishing in the county six vessels, manned by twenty-eight men; and fifty boats manned by forty-three men; of nets and seines there were in all a hundred and forty-one."

LIFE AT THE SHORE   Life at Morden was typical of the times with subsistence living key to survival. Fishermen were farmers and farmers were fishermen. Family was all important. Father and son worked the fields and woodlot and went to sea; mother and daughter tended to a myriad of domestic chores and kept the farm running when men folk were away. Some Bay Shore residents probably went to pick Valley apples or work in the evaporators and processing plants to make extra money.

SEA SIDE PARK HOTEL, HARBOURVILLE, C.1915

Harbourville was another of the Bay Shore villages that suffered from the loss of its lucrative export-import trade to the railroad. Tourism helped fill some of that void and by August 1904, the *Berwick Register* informed readers that "the two hotels here, Hillside and Clifton, are at present filled to overflowing with tourists, while many more are entertained in private houses…The people of Harbourville are a very social and friendly community…[and] take a deep and abiding interest in the welfare and affairs of the summer boarder." In 1909, a consortium of investors known as the Harbourville Realty Company purchased a small Harbourville hotel and cottages with plans to open a refurbished, enlarged upscale resort known as Sea Side Park. Heading the venture were three men—manager and controlling partner E. W. Kappele from Halifax; president Percy Gifkins, General Manager of the D. A. R. in Kentville; vice-president Sir Frederick Borden, long-time M. P. for Kings County and then Minister of Militia. When it opened in 1910, everything about Sea Side Park was grand, starting with its location on the summit of a ravine opposite McBride Bluff, two hundred and fifty feet above the beach with sweeping panoramic views from balconies and covered verandas. The lodge itself measured 151 feet by 28 feet with thirty-two rooms on the ground floor. The dining room, or tavern as it was called, had walls of oak wainscoting and colonial ceilings. Sea Side Park advertised a "large fleet of boats" for guests to enjoy cruises or deep-sea fishing; the steam packet *Ruby L* from neighbouring Margaretsville was chartered for "moonlight excursions" with dancing and the ever-popular ice cream social. Prices were set at twenty-five cents a person to encourage "liberal patronage" and Valley residents were welcomed to take part. Orchestras, "illuminated grounds," and "elegant suppers" were regular fare at Sea Side Park with management reserving the right to "exclude all objectionable persons." Wealthy American patrons from the eastern seaboard were preferred, and recruited by Kappele on frequent trips to Boston, but locals were not excluded from dropping in for a meal; on one occasion in 1913, more than one hundred made the boat trip across the Minas Channel from Advocate, Spencer's Island, and Port Greville. Sea Side Park was built with the intention "to play a conspicuous part in the future history of Nova Scotia as a vacation centre." On October 30, 1929, it became just that—part of history—when fire burned the three-storey, uninsured building to the ground.

HARBOURVILLE   The *Berwick Register*, August 25, 1897, reported: "Harbourville has become very popular as a summer resort, and is full of visitors." Harbourville's population steadily declined after the railway came through the Valley, dropping from 1,557 in 1871 to only 345 by 1901.

HARBOURVILLE, 1880S   Rens Spaans, a Bostonian, took this picture at Harbourville in the 1880s. Posing with the day's catch are three fishing buddies (Left to right: Bill Kreekele, Wall Skinner and Will Skinner).

CHARLIE MacDONALD'S CONCRETE HOUSE, CENTREVILLE, 1942

Charlie MacDonald (1874-1967), the "concrete man," wore many hats—adventurer, artist, innovator, social activist, eccentric. He was born at Steam Mill Village, Kings County—his father an apple grower, his grandfather a Presbyterian minister. Neither of these vocations interested him as much as art, his continual sketching in class driving teachers to despair. Charlie left school when he was fifteen, apprenticing first as a coffin maker, then as a wheelwright. Wanderlust got the better of him in 1898, and he went to sea as a carpenter during the waning days of tall ships. He travelled the world from Murmansk to Gibraltar to India, then returned to Canada and lived in British Columbia for several years. In 1912, he came home to Nova Scotia and opened a cement brick factory in Centreville just north of Steam Mill Village. Although concrete had been around since the Romans and was widely used in the 1850s, local people laughed him off. MacDonald persevered through the slow times (living in a tent beside the factory) until World War I drove demand for concrete through the roof, enabling him to build a new facility at Yoho outside Kentville. While living in Vancouver, Charlie had joined the Socialist Party of Canada. Disdainful of capitalism, he made the company, Kentville Concrete Products, a cooperative with his workers. In 1916, he married Mabel Meisner from Chipman's Brook who helped him convert the old factory into a cement house complete with cement bathtub, cement window sills and ornamental cement deer on his lawn. Now a museum, its architectural design was influenced, some say, by Charlie's South American and Mediterranean travels. Charlie and Mabel spent their summers camping at Huntington Point on the Bay of Fundy. When the Depression hit and business dried up, Charlie used what money he had saved to hire his destitute workers to build five cottages at the shore out of iron-reinforced cement, beach stone, and driftwood. The make-work project went on from 1934 to 1938, with Charlie owning one of the cottages and renting the others out to vacationers. In 1951, at seventy-seven years of age, he walked into Kentville Concrete Products, threw the keys to the foreman and said, "It's yours." Charlie MacDonald spent most of his remaining days at Huntington Point. A self-taught and accomplished artist, the hundreds of Valley and Cape Breton paintings and sketches he produced are considered "an invaluable record of his Nova Scotia."

CHARLIE MACDONALD AND ONE OF HIS COTTAGES, 1950S

One of five concrete and stone cottages built by Charlie MacDonald at Huntington Point during the Depression. Black and white images cannot do justice to the red, green, blue, and yellow hues Charlie incorporated into his creations.

CHARLIE MACDONALD AND HIS "TEA POT COTTAGE," 1950S

The unique structure was destroyed in 1982 but the other four "Gnome Homes" are still used today.

Hall's Harbour is named for pirate Samuel Hall, who was born in Kings County but left to fight on the side of the American Revolutionaries. He returned to the Bay Shore in 1779 as a privateer intent upon pillaging the area. Driven off by local militia, tales of Hall's buried treasure persist to this day. In July 2005, Bucknam Park was officially opened at Hall's Harbour to honour Ransford Dodsworth Bucknam, a native son whose intriguing life story is grounded in fact rather than legend. Ransford was born at Hall's Harbour in 1866, his family one of the first to settle there forty years earlier. When he was eight years old, both parents died unexpectedly and he went to live with his paternal grandparents, first in Hantsport, then in Winnipeg. At fourteen, Ransford signed on with a Great Lakes freighter and within two years had worked his way up to quartermaster on a schooner headed to the Pacific. While in Manila, the vessel's captain and mate died of cholera, leaving Ransford to assume command under a master's certificate granted before a hastily convened board of examiners. By the 1890s, Ransford had married and was living in Castine, Maine, where he captained a freighter in the coastal trade. While in Philadelphia having his vessel overhauled, Ransford was approached by the owner of Cramp's shipyard, who offered him a job delivering the first of four revenue cutters built for the Turkish government. Ransford accepted, and when the vessel *Medjida* arrived at Constantinople it was greeted by Turkey's ruler, Sultan Abdul Hamid II. The Sultan was so taken with Ransford he also made him an offer to be in charge of the Imperial revenue service. Ransford would be paid a $15,000 U. S. annual salary plus added benefits of a house, harem, and title of Admiral Bucknam Pasha. The deal was too good to pass up and by 1902 he had risen to vice-admiral of the empire. The only glitch in an otherwise fairy-tale story was that Ransford was married. He kept his spouse at home for a lengthy period saying Turkey was no place for a western woman, but as tales of infidelity filtered back, she went in search of him. What transpired upon her unannounced arrival is not known, but within a month, Ransford had vacated his post and returned to the United States. In 1916, the reconciled couple paid a return visit at the invitation of the Turkish government. Ransford was again offered command of the navy but he declined, thinking it better to keep his distance, since World War I was in full swing and Turkey had aligned with Germany. Bucknam Pasha died at Constantinople in 1919 under what some have called "mysterious circumstances."

CAPE SPLIT

LITTLE SPLIT ROCK At the southern entrance to Minas Basin on the tip of North Mountain's hook-shaped Blomidon Peninsula lies Cape Split. Accessible only by boat or a sixteen-kilometre hiking trail, it is here the Bay of Fundy flexes its awe-inspiring muscle. Reverberating across the top of the cliffs at mid-tide comes a "hollow roar" known as the "voice of the moon" (a reference to lunar forces), which is caused by a wall of water four storeys high rushing over submerged ridges hundreds of metres below. For ninety years, engineers and scientists have explored and discussed the feasibility and ramifications of harnessing the tides here to produce hydroelectric power. In 2005, Cape Split was identified as one of seven Bay of Fundy sites considered appropriate for possible future testing of a prototype underwater tidal-power turbine.

ISLE HAUTE, BAY OF FUNDY

Lying nineteen kilometres off the coast is a lava formation known as Isle Haute. Visible from many points along the Bay Shore, the basalt rock formation may have been part of the mainland until the Bay of Fundy was formed eight thousand years ago. Isle Haute (meaning high island) in all likelihood was named in 1604 when Champlain paid a brief visit. There is no evidence to suggest the island has ever been inhabited except for the island's lighthouse, which was first built in 1878. However, stone artifacts dating back one thousand years have turned up on the beach and legend contends Mi'kmaq and Maliseet warriors feasted on dog meat there three centuries ago before attacking the English at Annapolis Royal. During the late 1800s, the island was a favourite destination for summer boat excursions, some groups of picnickers numbering in the hundreds. On clear days, the 205-acre island with its three-hundred-foot cliffs topped by a carpet of forest green stands out in bold relief against the horizon. In a summer haze, it can appear half the size, then vanish like a ghost when fog shrouds the Bay of Fundy. Given its relative isolation, Isle Haute is understandably steeped in mystery and folklore, with plenty of tales of smuggling and ghostly fire ships. Then there are the tales of buried pirate loot, which rings of some truth. Between 1923 and 1936, treasure hunter Dougal Carmichael of Vancouver made several forays to the island. Using a map supposedly drawn by pirate Edward Low, he reportedly dug up twenty thousand dollars worth of coins taken in 1725 from the Spanish galleon *Senora de Victoria*. Edward Rowe Snow, a noted American marine historian and author, purchased the treasure map from Carmichael in 1947 and five years later paid his own visit to Isle Haute. Newspaper accounts of the time claim he was not disappointed. The partial skeleton of a man clutching eight doubloons was unearthed. Valued at $1,100, Snow left a happy man, probably making more on the story he wrote in one of his many adventure books than he did from the grisly find. Isle Haute today is federally owned with access limited unless authorized by the Canadian Coast Guard. In recent years, scientists from the Nova Scotia Museum have undertaken studies of its natural history, and future plans may involve designating the island a National Wildlife Area. Bay Shore communities suffering from a collapse of the fishery in recent years are also hopeful of promoting Isle Haute for ecotourism.

Chapter 5

Valley Gold

STARRS POINT, KINGS COUNTY

For all its attributes, the Valley's signature trademark remains the apple. Horticulture was introduced to the New World in 1606 at Port Royal where the French planted gardens of herbs, vegetables, and grain. Within four years, the fledgling colony was cultivating apple trees. As the Acadians migrated east to Minas Basin in the 1700s so, too, did the orchards. At the time of the Deportation, apples were well established in the Valley, as were pears, cherries, plums, peaches, quinces, vines, and currants. Planters and Loyalists bearing surnames of Spurr, Starr, Inglis, Burbidge, DesBarres, and Ruggles fostered the Acadian fruit legacy. It was Charles Prescott however, "Father of the Apple Industry," who elevated apple cultivation to a science with his studies of grafting techniques in the early 1800s while living at Starrs Point. This chapter, Valley Gold (the title borrowed from Anne Hutten's definitive book on the apple industry), is but a vignette of a centuries-old story that continues to evolve with the changing times.

JOSEPH KINSMAN
ORCHARD,
LAKEVILLE, KINGS
COUNTY, C.1911

In 1911, there were 2.5 million apple trees in the Valley. Apples were once a staple of the family larder. They were pressed into cider and vinegar, pared, sliced, and dried during peeling frolics or squirrelled away fresh in barrels for winter stock. Surplus was sold or traded locally for necessities, and culls (inferior fruit) fed to cattle. The few trees every farm planted were generally on difficult-to-plow hillsides, the better land reserved for root crops, grains, and cattle. As the science of apple growing evolved and orchards sprouted up throughout the Valley, there developed a need to market the bountiful harvests. In 1849, Ambrose Bent from Paradise, Annapolis County, and Benjamin Weir of Halifax exported the first load of Nova Scotia apples overseas from Halifax to Liverpool, England, earning two dollars a barrel for their efforts. Bent shipped seven hundred barrels to Boston in 1856, "the first to that market in any quantity, realizing about $2.75 per barrel." He continued his pioneering ways in 1881, teaming up with Benjamin Starratt from Paradise to be the first in sending apples (6,800 barrels) directly to London by steamer from Annapolis Royal, even travelling with the cargo to supervise its sale. As the railway was built through the Valley in the late 1800s, the apple industry gradually shifted eastward into Kings and Hants Counties and thus closer to Halifax's deep water piers, which held a decided advantage over the tide-dependent Valley ports. By 1890, apple exports to Britain totalled 100,000 barrels, an impressive statistic but one that paled compared to 1911 when 1.7 million barrels were shipped. Numbers continued to climb, topping 2 million barrels shipped in 1919, and peaking in 1933, when nearly 3.7 million barrels were exported, all but four hundred thousand going to Britain, the rest earmarked for domestic use and markets in Cuba, France, Belgium, and the Netherlands. Farmers sold their crops either on consignment to British brokerage houses and awaited payment or directly to local speculators who invariably offered a lower price. Either way, Valley apples ended up at large buyer auctions in Britain where the contents from a single barrel dumped out for display determined the price a grower received for his entire lot. Consumer preference for a particular apple was ever changing, which resulted in more than 160 varieties being grown by the 1930s. Markets were also unpredictable; a barrel of apples in London might return fifty cents one year and three dollars the next.

**BARRELS OF
GRAVENSTEIN
APPLES AT
RALPH EATON'S
HILLCREST
ORCHARDS,
KENTVILLE,
C.1901**

By 1892, twenty-five thousand acres of the Valley were covered in orchards.
Many claim apples were the catalyst for building a railway. A 1908 article
from the *Berwick Register* stated, "The Gravenstine [sic] has perhaps accomplished more than any other one apple to make Nova Scotia's reputation as an
apple growing country. Annapolis Valley Gravenstines carry an aroma and flavor seldom, if ever, equalled in any other apple grown here."

**PORT OF HALIFAX
SHOW, 1948**

The Valley in the early 1900s was "the apple orchard of the British Empire."
Nova Scotia apples were first displayed at London's Crystal Palace Fruit Show
in 1860 and 1862, resulting in a lucrative export trade with Britain that lasted
until World War II. Besides Gravensteins, other varieties "grown to a considerable extent" by 1900 included Ribston, King, Bishop Pippin, Baldwin, Cox's
Orange Pippins, Northern Spy, Greenings, and Russets.

APPLE WARE-HOUSE AT WOODVILLE, KINGS COUNTY, 1946

Subscribing to the adage of strength in numbers, Valley apple growers began organizing community-based cooperative fruit companies in the early 1900s to reduce freight costs and receive a better return for crops. They took charge of packing, shipping, and selling, thereby cutting out middlemen who had long profited at their expense. The first cooperative was the Berwick Fruit Company established in 1908 by twelve growers. That same year, legislation was passed creating the Farmers Fruit Produce and Warehouses Association Act, which authorized apple growers to manage their own affairs, from building storage facilities to marketing produce to buying supplies. Cooperatives sprang up from Windsor to Annapolis Royal, with eleven operating by 1910. A parent cooperative, the United Fruit Companies of Nova Scotia, was organized in 1912, and grew from thirty-two companies in 1913 to forty-nine in 1922. Each grower retained ownership of his apples and tried as best he could to keep track of inventory. To minimize costs, a cooperative member volunteered a certain number of hours to pack apples which often translated to young boys working off their father's commitment, sometimes ten hours a day, all winter, for no pay. Apples were packed as close to their shipping date as possible. Appearance was everything—the money a grower received depended upon how his apples were handled from picking, to sorting, packing, transporting, storing, stowing, and shipping. The Dominion and Nova Scotia Departments of Agriculture conducted a study in 1934 and 1935, tracking seven apple shipments from Valley orchards to British auction houses. Input was received from local fruit companies, the Dominion Atlantic Railway, Halifax Harbour Commission and Halifax Cold Storage Plant, Cunard-White Star Ltd., Furness Withy Ltd., London warehouses, and fruit brokers. A twelve-page farmers' bulletin *The Packing and Transportation of Nova Scotia Apples* was published in 1936 detailing how the "problems connected with handling Nova Scotia apples are numerous and complex." Included were many observations and recommendations concerning, among other issues, storage temperatures, barrel construction, preference of sling types for loading and unloading ships, and the advantages of moving barrels at dockside on carts instead of rolling them. Even the number of times a barrel was shaken to settle apples while packing drew attention.

**WAREHOUSE
PACKING ROOM,
C.1910**

Paid workers earned fifteen cents an hour; some men picked apples for ten hours, then packed for another ten hours to fill orders. There was no union work here; foremen were taskmasters, with some not permitting packers to talk. For quality control and identification purposes, the lid of each barrel bore the fruit company's name, the orchard from which the apples came, date packed, and number of the man who packed it.

**LOADING APPLES
INTO BOXCARS AT
BERWICK**

A single boxcar held three hundred barrels and during peak fall months when trains ran daily, stevedore gangs were brought in from the French shore. In winter, boxcars called reefers were used, which carried two hundred barrels; the claim is that eleven men once loaded a reefer in twenty minutes. During cold months, men travelled in the cars to run stoves that prevented apples from freezing on their way to Halifax for shipment.

**APPLE
WAREHOUSES
LINE THE
RAILWAY
TRACKS AT
BERWICK**

In this panorama of Berwick looking west, the five large buildings along the main railway track were apple warehouses; the smallest building (to the right of the tracks in the back) was the train station. Featured to the immediate right of the main tracks were the warehouses of (moving from foreground to background) Sam Chute and the Pleasant Valley Fruit Company. Warehouses to the immediate left of the tracks included (from foreground to background) P. L. Morse, F. A. Parker, and Berwick Fruit Company. The Berwick Fruit Company cooperage (not shown) was located south of the warehouse buildings. Other buildings of note include the boarding house also belonging to Berwick Fruit Company (the most westerly three-storey building in distance).

By 1930, there were 150 frost-proof warehouses in the Valley (sixty-nine cooperatively owned), with a total storage capacity of 1.6 million barrels. Warehouses were generally built to specifications—two storeys high and measuring one hundred feet by forty feet. It is widely accepted that on the Cornwallis Valley Railway between Kingsport and Kentville there was one warehouse for every kilometre of track. Some communities had several, such as Lakeville with four, Lawrencetown with five, and Kingston with seven. The large building with the smokestack in the foreground (far left), was an apple evaporator or dehydrator, an industrial-sized version of traditional peeling frolics. Evaporators were widely used and provided much-needed employment,

especially during the "Dirty Thirties," when women from as far away as Yarmouth came into the Valley to board and work. As many as three dozen men and women might be employed at a single evaporator. Men fed coal into drying furnaces, turned apples on the kiln floor, and packed fifty-pound boxes for shipment. Women peeled, cored, and sliced the apples by machine, standing for ten hours a day with no breaks, six days a week, for two dollars per day. About twelve hundred to fifteen hundred pounds of evaporated apples could be produced in a day. It was hard-earned money but a good wage considering the average labourer in the woods and sawmills earned ten cents an hour. Evaporated apples wholesaled in 1908 for seven cents a pound and for eight or nine cents a pound retail. This particular evaporator and adjacent warehouse shipped dried apples to Germany and Britain and was operated by R. V. Graham of Belleville, Ontario, who also owned warehouses at Kingston, Lakeville, Kentville, and Windsor. Generally built of wood and saturated in fruit sugars, evaporators were firetraps in the days before drying technology improved. No one can say with certainty how many there were as most were destroyed by fire. In 1921, evaporators produced approximately 455,000 kilograms (one million pounds) of dried apples; the number jumped to nearly six million kilograms (thirteen million pounds) in 1943, with one-half sent to England for the war effort. R. W. DeWolfe's in Wolfville, which closed in 1968, was thought to have been the last operational evaporator in Canada. Loss of the British market in World War II, combined with a switch to processing and the use of trucks for hauling in the 1950s, closed down most warehouses. Demolished or boarded up, a few are still used for apples in some places, as in Berwick, or have been converted into stores, as in Kingston and Wolfville.

Every community connected to the apple industry has at least one family name that stands out. Berwick, touted as the "Apple Capital of Nova Scotia," had the Chutes, of which three have been inducted into the local apple museum hall of fame. Sam Chute, pictured here, was the largest fruit producer of his day. In 1909, he sold four thousand barrels of apples, the largest single crop ever grown to that time. Although he served as first general manager of the cooperative United Fruit Companies of Nova Scotia, the "Apple King," as he was known, remained an independent, forming S.B. Chute Co. Ltd., which consisted of orchards, storage, and packing facilities. At his peak, Sam owned three hundred acres of orchard and produced forty thousand barrels of apples in addition to thirty thousand boxes of strawberries. During the 1890s, he is credited with pioneering the commercial use of fertilizer in the Valley. On January 20, 1910, the *Berwick Register* printed the following letter from Durban, South Africa: "While walking through the street of this city today I saw the following placard displayed in a shop window: Fit for a King, Choice Nova Scotia Apples, Kings, 8/6 Per Dozen [$1.02]. They were nice looking apples. I bought one for six pence. It tasted good I assure you, and while eating it my thoughts went back across the thousands of miles of water to our fair valley, where it was grown. I could not see any of Sam Chute's spray on the apples, but could see the effect of his fertilizer. Yours truly, E. F. Robbins. December 5, 1909."

Sam was noted for his civic mindedness especially in regards to a very generous contribution of ten thousand dollars he made in the 1920s toward the Berwick hospital building fund. Foster Chute, from nearby Waterville and a brother of Sam's, was an ardent supporter of the cooperative movement and instrumental in forming the United Fruit Company of Nova Scotia. Foster helped establish the Waterville Fruit Company, one of the Valley's largest cooperatives, and also operated F. M. Chute Fruit Company and Son.

John N. Chute (1867-1956), a cousin of Sam and Foster, is best remembered not as a grower but a builder of the apple industry. John was the first manager of the Berwick Fruit Company in 1908, a position which paid sixty dollars a month. He resigned in 1912 to work for the parent cooperative United Fruit Company of Nova Scotia, then became manager again of the Berwick Fruit Company in 1918 for the princely annual salary of fifteen hundred dollars. He spent time in London overseeing apple shipments before resigning from the Berwick Fruit Company in 1923. In the 1930s, John took up farming again, founding the Berwick Nursery Company Ltd., where he not only produced strawberries but strawberry plants for sale to other growers.

Two Valley innovators proved there is truth in the old saying that necessity is the mother of invention. In 1898, Benjamin Sanford of Woodville, Kings County, designed and patented an apple-picking basket that opened from the bottom, which minimized bruising when fruit was emptied into barrels. The *Berwick Register* reported on August 31, 1898, that "Mr. J. H. Cox [from Cambridge, Kings County] has purchased the patent right for Nova Scotia of the celebrated apple basket… He expects to go over the apple growing section of the province and introduce the basket."

The second invention of note was the Evangeline Apple Grader, designed and manufactured by Berwick's J. W. Hutchinson. An excerpt from an issue of the 1927 *Berwick Register* reads:

> The grader is constructed for grading all sizes of apples, from culls to large size No. one… It has a capacity for handling from 250 to 300 barrels of apples per day, depending upon the quality of the fruit. A machine of double capacity of about 500 barrels per day [was] specially constructed for the Berwick Fruit Company's large warehouse. The grader is operated by a one-half h.p. electric motor. The apples are fed into the machine from a bin of three barrel capacity, by means of an elevator operated by an endless belt. Another endless belt carries them through an alleyway from whence they pass beneath rollers specially gauged for eliminating the various sizes, each size or grade passing into a separate compartment onto a spacious sorting table, where they are sorted and picked over by the operators. Hoppers are placed at intervals along the table into which are deposited all culls. These drop through onto an endless belt and as they are carried forward to the receptacles that await them, are separated automatically into paring and older grades. The grader occupies a floor space of 27 x 8 feet… Mr. Hutchinson is to be congratulated on his ability and success in inventing, manufacturing and perfecting a grader of this type which has given such splendid satisfaction. Indeed the consensus of opinion of all connected with the fruit industry of the Annapolis Valley, who have seen it in operation, is that the "Evangeline" grader has all makes of imported apple graders entirely outclassed, not only in first cost but in economy of operation and capacity of output.

APPLES AT MANNING AND CYRUS ELLS'S FARM, PORT WILLIAMS, KINGS COUNTY, 1921

Manning and Cyrus Ells of Port Williams were one of about 150 buyers or speculators in the 1920s who purchased apples from Valley farmers and shipped them to England. While the operation in this photo looks impressive, it paled in comparison to that of William Henry Chase, also of Port Williams, who shipped two hundred thousand barrels a year. Chase was the undisputed "king" of all independent buyers. In 1885, he built the first trackside warehouse in the Valley at Port Williams. He owned four stores in the village, a cooperage, fertilizer plant, and insecticide warehouse. In the 1930s he constructed an evaporator and apple juice factory and by the 1950s was raising two hundred thousand poultry. Chase mentored a young Roy Jodrey from Hantsport when the future industrialist was only a teenager and worked for him buying apples. Harry Bruce writes of W. H. Chase: "Nova Scotians referred to him with the special awe some reserve for anyone who just might be the richest man in the province." A quoted source pretty much sums up the saying about the rich getting richer and the poor getting poorer: "Chase was the millionaire... He was the Bank of Canada around here. He owned everything and everybody... Chase had mortgages on a lot of the farms so he got their apples... He was probably one of the biggest financial wheels in the country and the way he manipulated the apple industry, other people made a living out of it but he made money out of it." Bruce credits the development

of Port Williams to four men—W. H. Chase, George Chase, Roy Jodrey and J. L. Illsley. George Chase, a nephew of W. H., was no slouch when it came to making money or taking charge if the situation warranted. In 1928, steamship companies such as Furness Withy threatened Valley buyers with a twenty cent per barrel markup on carrying fees (from 90 cents to $1.10) if they, as a group, did not agree to send apples through Halifax shippers. George Chase would have none of that. Instead, he enlisted the help of J. L Illsley, federal politician for Kings County, in persuading the Canadian government to construct a pier at Port Williams for apple shippers. It took some doing on Illsley's part, but the 230-foot cement wharf was built and with chartered vessels from Britain, Scandinavia, and Germany, Valley apples sailed out of Port Williams. Chase even went to Germany in the 1930s and met with Hitler to broker a deal to sell apples in return for fertilizer, a move not looked upon favorably by Valley residents. Chase and others certainly made their money but all Valley growers benefitted immensely from the millions of dollars saved in freight and shipping charges. In the fall of 1936, observers claimed a convoy of six thousand trucks stretching for twenty miles brought apples into Port Williams (an exaggeration, no doubt, but effective for proving the importance and scope of operations). When W. H. Chase died in the 1960s, his obituary in the Halifax *Chronicle Herald* called him "a Valley Giant, a member of the colourful company of rugged and restive individualists who helped to gain for the Maritimes a special niche in history's halls of commerce."

It cannot be said with certainty who first canned apples in the Valley for commercial use. Herb, Theodore, and William Smith owned Acadia Cannery at Kingston in 1902, which manufactured 1,100 cans a day for apples that were packed, six cans to a case, and shipped to Winnipeg, Vancouver, and London, England. D. F. Webber, the United States Consul General at Halifax in 1908, mentions in a report on the apple industry of Nova Scotia that evaporators "run canneries and in this way dispose of a large amount of the fruit. The apples for canning are peeled and cored, quartered, and four and one-half to five pounds are put into a gallon (No. 10) can. Most of the machines [are] made by a firm of Rochester, N. Y. These cans are sealed and submerged in boiling water from five to seven minutes. This thoroughly heats the contents, but not to such an extent that the fruit becomes soft or mushy. These wholesale for $2 per dozen gallon cans." By the 1940s, scores of workers at Valley plants were running machines that pared, cored, mashed, fermented, canned, bottled, and packaged nine thousand barrels of apples a day. An array of products and by-products came off the lines including cider, wine, vinegar, juice, concentrate, pomace, pectin, essence, flakes, butter, sauce, pie filling, jams, and jellies.

APPLES USED AT
M. W. GRAVES &
CO., INGLEWOOD
ROAD,
BRIDGETOWN

In the 1880s, Minard Graves moved from Port Lorne on the Bay Shore to Granville where he began making vinegar with a hand press at Vinegar Hill Farm. He expanded operations to Upper Granville in 1893 to manufacture cider vinegar. With sons Francis and Owen joining the business, Minard built this apple juice and concentrate-processing plant and evaporator at Bridgetown in 1901, where he also continued to make his by-then famous cider vinegar. When American Robert Steppanski's grandiose plans for a distillery in Berwick failed to materialize in the 1930s, Minard purchased the factory following a sheriff's sale and moved operations there, later selling his Bridgetown property, ironically, to L. J. McGuinness for a distillery (see Chapter 3). The Berwick plant was operated as a subsidiary of M.W. Graves under the name Berwick Fruit Products Limited, and processed apples, pears, and strawberries. By 1940, Graves was turning out ten thousand cans of apple juice a day and had begun making apple sauce, the first such venture in the Maritimes. The cooperatively owned United Fruit Companies of Nova Scotia also had a plant in Berwick and another at Aylesford. In one year, the two Berwick operations together went through 113,000 barrels of apples, employed nearly 250 people, and paid $2,400 in weekly wages.

There were other apple processors. Just up the road at Waterville was a small cannery owned by O'Leary and Lee. Middleton had two; the first opened in 1929 after Horton Phinney acquired a jam and jellies plant at Cambridge, operated by R. W. Arengo-Jones under the name Scotian Gold, and moved the equipment to Middleton. Eventually, with Horton's son Norman managing the business, Scotian Gold became a household name, turning out a variety of apple products. In 1945, when United Fruit Companies of Nova Scotia bought out the Phinneys, Scotian Gold employed 425 people and shipped six railcar loads of canned apples a day for overseas. The second Middleton plant was opened in 1935 by Canadian Canners Ltd. from Hamilton, Ontario, which processed peas, apples, and pears under the Aylmer brand name. (When Del Monte took over Canadian Canners in the late 1950s, the Middleton facility was closed down.) In 1946, Kent Foods Ltd. of Canning began producing vinegar and Allen's brand apple juice. The last big name to enter the apple processing business was Roy Jodrey, who opened a juice plant in his home town of Hantsport in 1947, then two years later purchased another in Port Williams where he established Annapolis Valley Canners, later known as Avon Foods Ltd. By the early 1980s, Graves and Avon Foods were using over half of all the apples grown in the Valley.

BRIDGETOWN CO-OP, C.1949

Webster's Dictionary defines cooperative as "an enterprise or organization owned by and operated for the benefit of those using its services." Cooperatives were born during the Industrial Revolution in England when workers and consumers joined forces to circumvent unscrupulous merchants who provided low-quality goods and services at inflated prices. In the days of sail, fishing schooners were often built and manned by a cooperative of investors who shared the profits and risks. The first business cooperative in North America was established at Stellarton in 1861 by migrant British coal miners. There are more than four hundred cooperatives providing goods and services of all descriptions in Nova Scotia today with one in three Nova Scotians said to be a co-op member. Agricultural cooperatives are the most numerous, covering the spectrum from fruit and vegetable producers to dairies, livestock, poultry processing, and farm supplies. One of the first cooperative farm stores was opened in 1915 at Halifax by the United Fruit Companies of Nova Scotia, which sold vegetables, fruits, butter, and eggs. Once common throughout the Valley and considered "part of a community's fabric," most co-op stores like Bridgetown's have disappeared in the face of giant retailers. Unfortunately the people in the descriptive images at right are unidentified. The displays, however—everything from chocolates to washing machines to farm machinery advertisements—provide an insightful glimpse at the diversity of products made available to rural communities through co-op stores.

BRIDGETOWN CO-OP, C.1949

Windsor's 1953 Apple Blossom parade float

Postcard of float entered by town of Windsor in 1953 Apple Blossom Festival Parade depicting Judge Thomas Haliburton and his wife being chauffeured by "Sam Slick the Clockmaker." The statuesque horse stood for years after in the window of a Windsor store.

Attending the 73rd Apple Blossom Festival in 2005 was ninety-eight-year-old Kentville resident Garth Calkin, one-time town mayor and drugstore owner. Mr. Calkin's presence was especially newsworthy because he was the last surviving member of a six-person organizing committee for the first Apple Blossom Festival staged in 1933. Then it was known as the Apple Blossom Carnival, a three-day pageant (now four days) intended to celebrate and promote the Valley's apple industry, cultural history, and natural beauty. The Associated Screen News from Montreal filmed the inaugural proceedings to air in movie theatres throughout Canada and the United States. Annually scheduled for the end of May as a kick-off to the tourist season, the widely popular attraction is now planned five years in advance to allow for the booking of celebrity performers. Except on the rare occasion when Wolfville, Kingston, or Windsor hosted the grand street parade, the festival has been staged in and around Kentville, the now defunct C. P. R. Cornwallis Inn being the long-time media headquarters and venue for social activities. Festival goals and format have remained relatively unchanged over the years. Princesses representing towns from Windsor to Digby vie for the title of "Queen Annapolisa," upwards of 150 entries including floats and marching bands make up one of Canada's largest street parades, and events for all ages highlight entertainment. An interesting side note occurred in 1945, when syndicated film producer James Fitzpatrick, whose "Voice of the Globe" movies sold throughout the world, brought a film crew to cover the coronation. For another promotional, a motion picture *Apple Blossom Wedding* was filmed with Miss Gladys Wade from Kentville playing the bride and Philip Donat the groom. Donat's brother was British film star Robert Donat (1905-1958) a cinematic heartthrob who won an Oscar for his 1939 role in *Goodbye Mr. Chips.* An Apple Blossom Festival connection with Hollywood remains to this day, as Philip Donat's son Peter, now living in San Francisco, was born in Kentville. He, too, went on to become a movie and television actor and has performed in recent years at the Atlantic Theatre Festival in Wolfville.

APPLE BLOSSOM PRINCESSES, N.D.

Internationally renowned Halifax photographer Wallace R. MacAskill took this picture of Apple Blossom princesses strolling through an orchard, possibly at Port Williams. Incorporated in 1935 by the provincial legislature, the festival has twice been selected by the American Bus Association as one of the top one hundred tourist events for North America. In 2002, the Royal Canadian Mint struck a commemorative fifty-cent sterling silver coin.

BETTY ANN WEST, PRINCESS BERWICK 1957

Betty Ann West, Princess Berwick 1957, acknowledges on-lookers at Kentville's Memorial Park during Apple Blossom festivities. To Mary Armour of Middleton goes the honour of being crowned the first Queen Annapolisa in 1933.

NOVA SCOTIA APPLE MARKETING BOARD PHOTO OF A DOMINION GROCERY STORE IN HALIFAX, 1948

Nova Scotia now ranks fourth in Canada for apple production behind British Columbia, Ontario, and Quebec, but some solace can be taken in knowing the Valley had orchards more than two hundred years before any of the other provinces. After World War II when Britain began planting apple trees and Valley exports died out, post-war farms took on a new look of "diversification" with smaller orchards and less apple varieties oriented toward processing.

Government paid farmers four dollars a tree to uproot acres of useless apples to make room for other fruits, vegetables, and livestock. Today, acreage under cultivation is down but volume is not, as new plantings are at a higher density and yield. Hundreds, possibly thousands, of varieties have come and gone over the centuries. Among the current favourites are Gravenstein, McIntosh, Cortland, Red Delicious, Golden Delicious, Spartan, Idared, Empire, Golden Russett, Honey Crisp, Northern Spy, Jonagold, Jersey Mac, Paula Red, and Cox's Orange. The variety of the future is considered to be Honeycrisp, with its crunchiness, aromatic flavour, high quality, and longer shelf life making it appetizing to a broader market. Costlier to grow but giving a better return on investment, one-tenth of Valley orchard land (six hundred acres) is currently being converted to Honeycrisp in a five-year make-over.

Nova Scotia grows 2.5 million bushels of apples annually (three bushels equivalent to the old barrel measurement), with more than ninety percent coming from Kings County. Apple pickers from across the province once came to "mine" the Valley's gold during harvest time. In recent years however, growers have become increasingly dependent upon migrant workers from Mexico, Barbados, and Jamaica for seasonal help. Most apples are now consumed locally although it is hoped a growing international appeal for Honeycrisp will reverse that trend. While apples are still juiced in the Valley under the traditional Graves and Allen's brand names, a whole new industry has opened up for the fresh and frozen pie-processing business. And connoisseurs of fine drink can still purchase Chipman's Golden Glow alcoholic apple cider. First brewed during Prohibition by Lewis Chipman out of his kitchen at Chipman's Corner, then manufactured in Kentville for many years, the once widely popular, low-cost beverage is still produced in-province using Valley apples.

Chapter 6

Soldiers of the Soil

COMMUNAL WORK PARTY

Communal work parties or frolics were once popular community events used for labour-intensive tasks such as barn raisings, clearing land, and harvesting crops. Farmers during World War I were referred to as "Soldiers of the Soil." In an open letter to the *Berwick Register* October 7, 1914, Premier G. H. Murray wrote: "No man occupies a more important place in the present crisis than the farmer. The food supplies available will probably enter into the final success more than any other condition. The farmer, therefore, who means to produce all the food supplies that he can on the farm during the next year is just as useful a patriot as the farmer who shoulders his gun and goes to war... Farmers of Nova Scotia, this is your hour of opportunity. A solemn duty has been laid upon your shoulders... Our kinsmen in the Motherland have to be fed, so do also the people of the countries devastated by war. You in peaceful Nova Scotia are now in a position to do much for the cause of humanity and for the enduring benefit of our Empire."

KENTVILLE EXPERIMENTAL STATION

The historical importance of farming to the Valley is exemplified in the fact that the Kings County Agricultural Society was organized as early as 1789, its broad mandate, according to Eaton's county history, being "the better improvement of husbandry, encouragement of manufactures, cultivation of the social virtues, acquirement of useful knowledge, and to promote the good order and well being of the community to which we belong." Involved in all manner of affairs from starting up Sunday schools to establishing libraries to fencing cemeteries, "one of the first acts of this society was the appointment of an agent in Halifax for the 'vending of beef, etc.' and the appointment in the county of inspectors, whose business it should be to see 'that cattle sent to the agent were fit for the market'... It [also] concerned itself with the buying of imported stock and seeds, making experiments in fertilizing land with marsh mud, lime and plaster, testing new or strange crops, holding fairs and plough-ing matches..." In 1843, the society had three branch associations in Horton, Cornwallis, and Aylesford Townships, a number that increased by 1898 to nine county-wide, with a total of 677 members. Similar societies were orga-nized during the same time period throughout the province, one being the Fruit Growers' Association and International Show Society of Nova Scotia, established in 1863 at Halifax. Until 1901, annual meetings were held at Wolfville, where in 1893 a school of horticulture was set up in conjunction with Acadia University. This initiative later turned into the Nova Scotia Fruit Growers' Association, which historians like Eaton believe was largely responsi-ble for the Valley's "remarkable success" in the fruit industry. The association also began lobbying the Dominion Government in 1895 to establish a "fruit experimental station" in the Valley. After many years of frustration, the deci-sion was finally reached in 1911 to acquire 250 acres of farm land in Kentville where the Kentville Experimental Station was established.

FLAILING TURNIP SEED AT KENTVILLE EXPERIMENTAL STATION, C.1918

Seeds of various kinds were imported into Canada from Europe for many years, but during World War I that supply line was severed. To compensate for the loss, more than thirteen tons of turnip seed were produced per year for local farmers at the Kentville Experimental Station and on additionally leased lands. The building in the distance was the superintendent's residence from 1912 to 1979. It now houses the Blair House Museum, which is named for the station's first superintendent, Dr. William Saxby Blair. Opened in 1982 under the auspices of the Nova Scotia Fruit Growers' Association, the museum focuses on the history of the apple industry and station.

KENTVILLE RAVINE

Approximately one hundred and forty acres of the original Experimental Station property consisted of forested ravine with trees two hundred years old. Established at the outset as a park where only natural selection is allowed, its trails are a favourite haunt of hikers and scientists. Featured here are members of the Kentville Board of Trade on a sleigh ride in 1913; three years later the park's main road was closed to traffic because of excessive litter.

ENTOMOLOGY FIELD LABORATORY, "INSECTICIDE INVESTIGATIONS FOR CANADA," ANNAPOLIS ROYAL, C.1915

Many of the early challenges faced by the fledgling Kentville Experimental Station were understandably addressed on a "trial and error" basis until research in scientific principles evolved. One area of concern receiving immediate attention was entomology. A small field laboratory was established at Bridgetown in 1911, then moved to Annapolis Royal four years later where it remained until 1952 when it transferred to Kentville. Apples and potatoes, being the Valley's two primary crops in the early 1900s, drew special attention from the outset. Tests were conducted comparing the merits of dusting and spraying. Various concoctions of insecticides and fungicides that would horrify today's environmentalists were applied to knock down a host of diseases and pests. Even then, issues were raised about the residual affect of chemical agents on plants and soils as well as human beings. In a letter to the *Berwick Register* addressing the problematic apple maggot or railroad worm in 1927, J. P. Spittall from the Dominion Entomological Laboratory told farmers, "Since the scare in England on account of arsenical residues on apples we are unable to recommend the use of lead arsenate which up to 1925 had proved to be the most efficient control." By the 1940s, entomological studies had advanced to where a "holistic ecological" approach was being tested "which drew world wide attention and is now [1986] considered a classic in research on insect control." There was much more to the Experimental Station than creepy crawlers and scabby blights. At Kentville, structures for a multitude of uses were built including barns, sheds, and pens. Acreage doubled and six private farms around the province were selected as "illustration stations" to demonstrate fertilizers, crop rotations, and crop varieties. More than three thousand fruit trees were cultivated on station grounds. Research programs were developed to include vegetables, small fruits, ornamentals, greenhouse crops, livestock, poultry, bees, forages, cereals, and field crops. Studies and tests were conducted for the food-processing sector in regard to canning and freezing fruits and vegetables. Since 1913, meteorological instruments have monitored Valley air temperatures, precipitation, wind, soil temperatures, and amount of sunshine. Now called the Kentville Research Station (under the auspices of Agriculture and Agri-Food Canada) the one-time pioneer is a recognized world leader in its field.

COMBINATION VAPORIZER AND DUST DISTRIBUTOR, ANNAPOLIS ROYAL

DUSTING POTATOES WITH A HAND SPRAYER, ANNAPOLIS ROYAL

COMBINATION GRAIN HARVESTER AND BINDER AT WORK NEAR LAKEVILLE, KINGS COUNTY, 1918

American historian Henry Adams wrote of early farm tools, "The machinery of production showed no radical difference from that familiar in ages long past. The Saxon farmer of the eighth century enjoyed most of the comforts known to Saxon farmers of the eighteenth." The early nineteenth century ushered in an Agricultural Revolution when an assortment of mechanized farm machinery made its appearance, the most heralded being the mechanical reaper (above). Harvesting grain was long considered the most demanding, backbreaking job on a farm. Wielding a reaping hook or sickle a farmer was fortunate to cut one acre of grain a day; using a scythe, production jumped to three acres a day. In 1831, inventor Cyrus Hall McCormick from Virginia eased the discomfort considerably with the world's first "commercially successful" mechanical reaper. Requiring only two men—one to ride the horse and another to rake grain from the platform—it performed the work of sixteen men with sickles. Improved models followed and by 1876, the McCormick Harvester and Binder cut and bound grain in one operation; fifty thousand were sold between 1877 and 1885. A few merchants in the Valley profited from selling farm machinery, including Walter M. Carruthers of Kentville who operated a dealership for the Deering Harvesting Machinery Company before it became part of International Harvester Company in 1902.

RARE PICTURE OF A PORTABLE OX-POWERED "ANIMAL ENGINE" TREAD-MILL, C.1888

GASOLINE POW-ERED THRESHING MACHINE, KENTVILLE EXPERIMENTAL STATION, 1928

An interesting contraption was the "animal engine" treadmill which was powered by horses, donkeys, or oxen to drive machines for pumping water, crushing ore, and threshing and grinding grain; smaller models designed for dogs, sheep, or goats churned butter and separated cream. Teamster Edward M. Skinner from the South Berwick area (above) probably travelled the countryside renting out his equipment and services. To operate Skinner's treadmill, he would have had to first unload the inclined box from the wagon, level it on supports, then attach a large side-mounted drive wheel and belts in much the same manner as pictured with the gasoline-powered engine (bottom right). The animal then entered the box by walking up a ramp at the rear and onto a large treadmill made of wooden slats forming a continuous chain. Once the animal began walking, a series of gears were set in motion, driving the wheel and belts that were hooked to the piece of equipment requiring power. Skinner's machine must have been an older model, as by the 1870s treads were horizontal rather than inclined, which provided a more solid footing for the animal and decreased leg strain.

**LOAD OF BARRELS
HEADED FOR THE
VALLEY**

Barrels were used in such quantities that Valley coopers couldn't always meet demand. Shipments were then brought in over the South Mountain from New Ross, Lunenburg County, first by wagon, then by truck such as the one featured here, which carried three hundred barrels in one trip. Apple growers alone sent millions of hardwood barrels to England and none came back, sometimes being sold off for a shilling (twelve cents) to help recoup shipping expenses. There were two kinds of barrels. Dry, or slack, barrels held apples, potatoes, flour, and grains; wet, or tight, barrels were for fish, molasses, vinegar, cider, and pickles. Apple barrels were federally inspected to ensure guidelines for specific measurements were followed. Every community had at least one cooperage and sawmill where staves (barrel slats) and headers (barrel ends) were manufactured. In 1891, fifty-six cooperages employed sixty-eight people in Annapolis County. There were big and small operations. Silas L. Gates of Port Williams produced ten thousand barrels a year while the town's apple mogul W. H. Chase turned out two hundred thousand. In 1919, thirty-four shareholders organized the North Kingston Company Ltd., a farmers' cooperative that among other ventures built barrels; members paid forty-five cents a barrel, non-members fifty-five cents, delivery included. Twelve coopers were kept busy turning out forty-five thousand barrels a year which were trucked to customers from Hantsport to Bridgetown. A spin-off business was the making of alder hoops (to hold barrels together) which were purchased for twelve dollars per thousand in the 1920s from people living on the North Mountain. Fire was always a threat in the early days. On October 3, 1933, Carl Smith opened a new cooperage at Aylesford; eighteen hours later the uninsured building burned to the ground along with five hundred barrels, twenty-two thousand staves, eleven thousand hoops, and ten thousand heads, resulting in a loss of four thousand dollars. On March 17, 1938, the International Coopers Union was organized at Berwick, the first of its kind in Canada. From an initial group of twenty-five, spearheaded by Holmes Keddy, membership soon swelled to more than two hundred. Working conditions and wages were the central issues. A cooper then was making fifty to sixty barrels a day and being paid anywhere from four to seven cents a barrel. It was argued at the time that a fair wage should be eight cents a barrel!

HANTSPORT FRUIT BASKET FACTORY

Barrels were used for flour until World War I when they were replaced by cotton bags, but apples continued to be shipped in barrels until the 1940s when wooden bushel boxes were introduced. These were never popular with farmers as picking baskets could not be emptied into one without bruising the fruit. The bushel box, however, remained the container of choice until the 1960s when a switch was made to eighteen-bushel bulk bins. In addition to barrels, there was always a great demand for small baskets, boxes, and crates for berries, butter, and cheese. One of the principal businesses for this line of wooden ware was the Hantsport Fruit Basket Company started in 1910 by D. W. Murray. In the beginning, strawberry boxes were produced but when blueberry shipments to Boston increased from 1910 to 1920, the Hantsport Fruit Basket Company was the first to supply thirty-two-quart wooden crates and veneer boxes. In 1928, the business turned out five hundred thousand boxes; by 1934, production had increased to eight hundred thousand.

THE TOWN OF BERWICK HELD A HORSE PULL AT ITS INAUGURAL GALA DAYS IN 1946, AN ATTRACTION THAT HAS REMAINED A PART OF THE ANNUAL FESTIVITIES FOR SIXTY YEARS

Horses and oxen have been a fixture of the Valley landscape for nearly four centuries. The French had horses at Port Royal Habitation in 1613, and history is full of references to the use of oxen by Acadians. Oxen were the early draft animal of choice whenever brute strength was needed for clearing and working land, hauling logs out of the woods, pulling supply wagons, grading and plowing roads, and moving buildings and vessels. It wasn't that oxen were better at it than horses, they were just cheaper to feed, required little in the way of care or equipment, and when they outlived their usefulness they could be slaughtered to be eaten or sold. Certain areas of Nova Scotia are associated with oxen more closely than others, the south and French shores being the two most noteworthy, perhaps reflective of their German and Acadian roots. In 1770, there were eighty-six horses in Annapolis County and 190 oxen, although there is no way of knowing how many horses were used for riding as opposed to working. With the introduction of heavy agricultural machinery in the mid-nineteenth century, demand for horses increased. Large draft breeds such as Percherons, Clydesdales, and Belgians were much sought after but since they were less plentiful here, many were imported from western Canada. Neither oxen nor horses are used much anymore for farm and woods work. Both can still be seen occasionally in action at county exhibitions and community fairs, where owners compete to see whose animals can pull the heaviest load the greatest distance. The earliest competitions took the form of ploughing matches which gave prizes for the "person who should stump and plow for crop the greatest quantity of land never plowed before, not more than three stumps per acre left on the land, and all stones that materially obstructed the operation of plowing and harrowing to be removed, the quantity to be not less than two acres."

**OX PULL,
LAWRENCETOWN
EXHIBITION,
1950S**

Today there are nineteen county or area exhibitions staged throughout Nova Scotia, many of which can trace their roots to the 1800s. Lawrencetown has been home to the six-day Annapolis County Exhibition—more recently called the Annapolis Valley Exhibition—since 1927. Its beginnings actually date to 1917 when a one-day United School Exhibition was organized at Lawrencetown's Demonstration Building with children from the school district submitting displays and entries of livestock, flowers, sewing, and essays. Now 241 years old, the Hants County Exhibition held in Windsor enjoys the distinction of being the first such event in North America. From an undated newspaper account, D. I. Scotney described Windsor's first agricultural fair as follows: "The first fair and market was held on May 21, 1765. At this show cattle, sheep, horses, hogs, butter, cheese, grain and homespun were shown. The prizes consisted of three yards of English blue superfine cloth, a pair of shears, a plow share, butter churn, buckskin breeches, spurs, whips, wool cards, laced hat, buckskin gloves, ribbon and medals. Entertainment was in the form of wrestling and shooting matches."

JACK PARR'S HORSE TRAILER, 1930s

Jack Parr of Middleton was possibly Nova Scotia's biggest buyer and seller of horse flesh. He used this car and trailer to make deliveries around Nova Scotia. Jack Parr was born in 1895 at Stewartsville, Missouri. In 1906, his father John accepted a land grant in Alberta and moved his family and mules to a farm at Castor, a prairie community that owed its beginnings to the railway. After a time, John and his two sons, Jack and Herschel, opened a Ford dealership selling tractors and other farm equipment. How Jack ended up in the Valley is a mystery. At different times during the Depression, he brought in a rail boxcar carrying upwards of eighteen horses to sell at Middleton. On one of his forays in 1936, he stayed and established operations at the eastern end of town in the vicinity of today's Big Scoop Restaurant. Western horses were free spirited but not wild; by local standards, however, they were considered a tad rough to handle and had to be tamed before being put out to work the fields and woods. Jack conducted numerous buying trips over the years to the prairie provinces, on occasion making headlines. In 1944, he set a western Canadian record at Calgary's annual spring horse sale forking out $350 for a purebred Percheron gelding, then paid the highest price ($590) for a pair of sorrel and chestnut Belgian geldings. Jack returned to Middleton from that trip with three railcars full of horses, ninety percent being Percherons, which his client preferred, he told reporters. The client on this occasion was possibly Bowater, an American pulpwood conglomerate with vested interests in both Nova Scotia and Newfoundland. Bowater's veterinarian, a Dr. Gould, often came to Middleton on horse business and stayed with the Parrs. In 1957, Bowater paid Jack one hundred thousand dollars for 280 horses (each weighing approximately 727 kilograms) which were sent in lots of five railcar loads, first to Sydney, Cape Breton, then on to Newfoundland by ferry, where they were used in the woods. Many local farmers purchased horses as well but some couldn't afford to keep them through the winter so Jack would buy them back, reportedly paying a fair price in the process. Citizens of Middleton still remember when men led horses four-in-hand from the train station through town. Jack left the business in 1959 as mechanization was taking over; he died on April 16, 1968, at the age of 73. There were other dealers in the horse trade but from all accounts, there was only one Jack Parr.

Jack Parr, centre right, on a horse-buying trip in western Canada

Curtis Guild Coleman worked for Jack Parr "taming" western horses before they were sold to local farmers and woods operators

**END OF AN ERA—
CHANGING
HORSEPOWER**

When the first steam-powered tractors appeared on the market in 1868, they were used for general haulage, primarily in the timber profession. Pictured above is a steam-driven tractor with threshing machine in tow, circa 1900; Hanley Palmer of Rockland (south of Berwick) stands at the controls with Robert Joudrey to the rear, possibly keeping an eye on boiler pressure. This is thought to have been the first self-propelled vehicle in western Kings County. Like Edward Skinner and his animal treadmill, Palmer travelled the countryside threshing farmers' grain.

FROM HAY BURNERS TO GAS GUZZLERS

At the Kentville Experimental Station, some very important-looking men watch intently as a gasoline powered No. 7 Oliver tractor pulling an eight-foot windrower gives a plowing demonstration. Note the non-rubberized, steel-treaded tires. When the station opened in 1911, there were six draft horses and a driving horse in use. By the time the first tractor arrived in 1919 (perhaps this very one), there were thirteen horses and a new barn had been built. Forty years later, all were sold. There were various tractor dealers in the Valley. G. N. Reagh and Sons of Middleton started in 1903 with horse-drawn International Harvester farm machinery, then introduced tractors in 1915, selling two the first year. In April 1921, Woodworth Bros. of Berwick advertised CASE kerosene tractors at pre-war prices with only limited numbers available for spring farm work. Also in the 1920s, Kentville's F. W. Robinson sold Fordson brand tractors.

SUCKING IT UP

When the labour-intensive, hand-block cutting and drying of peat moss on the Caribou Bog at Berwick was replaced by vacuum harvesters in 1954, annual production jumped from five thousand bales to fifty thousand.

DOUBLE-CROPPING

HARVESTING CORN FOR ENSILAGE

There was a time in Nova Scotia when most everyone farmed or was related to someone who did. Today, less than two percent of the population is employed in farming, yet agriculture creates sixteen thousand jobs and pumps one billion dollars annually into the provincial economy. During the late nineteenth and early twentieth centuries, "double-cropping" was a common practice to maximize land use. Vegetables, berries, and grains were planted between rows of apple trees. Potatoes, rutabagas (turnips), and dried beans were the main vegetables grown. Potatoes were number one, with approximately thirty thousand acres under cultivation in the early 1900s; eleven thousand acres were devoted to rutabagas, mangels, and sugar beets, much of which served as livestock feed. With the exception of these crops, until the 1920s there were only three or four hundred acres of farmland in the entire province committed to the commercial production of vegetables, everything until then being grown in small rural and urban gardens. Corn was used predominately for silage until the 1940s when sweet varieties increased in popularity, although demand as a table delicacy did not mushroom until thirty years later.

SEEDER, HARROW COMBO

Today, there are approximately four thousand farms in Nova Scotia encompassing one million acres in total, the average size about 250 acres. More than fifty varieties of vegetable crops are raised accounting for some thirty agricultural products exported to sixty countries worldwide, with fifty percent of exports going to the United States. Three out of every ten farms are located in the Valley, the highest percentage in the province. Kings County produces the widest range of crops and livestock of any farming region east of southern Ontario. One Valley cooperative of eight farms harvests 4,500 acres, ships twenty-five million pounds of mixed vegetables and fruit, and provides one hundred full-time and four hundred part-time jobs. Another cooperative of five companies, each with "member farms," has four hundred full-time and eight hundred part-time employees. In the late 1990s, there were at least thirty-seven "secondary establishments" in Kings County related to agricultural manufacturing. When all farm production is taken into account, Kings County, on a per capita basis, is nearly two and a half times the national average. Still, farming is not for the faint of heart or weak willed. Recent years have seen poor growing seasons, and agricultural reports continually show the price Nova Scotia's farmers receive for their products are outstripped by operational costs, leading many to depend upon crop insurance, government subsidies, and loans for their survival.

**PLANTING
POTATOES,
KINGS COUNTY**

Special varieties of potato are used for making chips, two grown in the Valley over the years being Superior and Kennebec. Since King's County produces two-thirds of Nova Scotia's potatoes, it seems only proper that the Mi'kmaq named this district *Sipekni'katik* meaning "wild potato." In 1867, Kings County was Canada's top potato-exporting region. Canning, Port Williams, Sheffield Mills, and farms along the top of the North Mountain were the biggest producers. The village of Canning, according to *The History of Kings County*, was built upon the potato industry. "Wagons and carts from all parts of the [Cornwallis] township loaded with potatoes filled the streets from morning till night, the vessels for their reception lying at the wharves as many as eleven deep."

Demand for these potatoes only increased with the invention of the potato chip, an invention that was made out of spite more than by design. The story goes that in 1853, Native American George Crum was working as a chef for an upscale resort in Saratoga Springs, New York. A guest returned one of Crum's french fry servings for being too thickly cut; a second offering was also rejected. The frustrated Crum retaliated by cooking up a batch of fries so paper thin and crispy they couldn't be eaten with a fork, but his plan backfired when the disgruntled customer loved them. Others, too, loved Crum's creation, and the potato chip was born. In 1860, Crum opened his own restaurant and within short order counted Vanderbilts and Hiltons among his clientele. The restaurant closed in 1890 and Crum passed away in 1914 at the age of ninety-two. In 1895, William Tappendon of Cleveland began selling potato chips in grocery stores, and many other companies went into production between 1908 and 1932. In 1932, C. E. Doolin of San Antonio opened Frito Company and Herman Lay of Nashville began distributing Lay's potato chips. In 1935, Edward Synder started Hostess potato chips, which was acquired in 1959 by General Foods. Frito Company arrived in Canada in 1958, merged into Frito-Lay in 1961, struck up a partnership with Hostess in 1987, and took over the company in 1992. Frito-Lay Canada has offices in Kentville and a potato chip plant near New Minas, one of six in Canada.

FINISHED POTATO CHIPS COMING OFF SCOTTIES PRODUCTION LINE

PACKAGING SCOTTIES POTATO CHIPS

Two brands of potato chips were produced in Nova Scotia during the 1950s—Tom Thumb (Glendale Foods) at Canning and Scotties at New Minas. Tom Thumb was short lived, going out of production after a plant fire in the early 1960s. Scotties began at Centreville, Kings County, in 1954, then moved to New Minas in 1959. The company was eventually taken over by Hostess of General Foods.

Bridgetown historian Elizabeth Coward credits R. C. Nutt with being the first vegetable processor in Nova Scotia. Nutt operated a factory at Bridgetown from 1881 to 1884 which canned tomatoes, corn, peas, and beans, along with blueberries, cherries, plums, and pears. Cans were supplied by an adjacent iron foundry, which turned out one thousand a day in addition to manufacturing harrows and plows. In 1884, fire destroyed both the foundry and cannery after which nothing more was heard of Nutt's enterprise. Herbert Oyler of Auburn is said to have been an early producer of canned pickles, tomato chow and cranberry sauce. Vegetable processing was slow to develop in the Valley until the 1930s when consumer demand grew for canned beans, peas, beets, carrots, cucumbers, and corn. As a result, acreage devoted to growing vegetables throughout Nova Scotia nearly doubled within ten years; World War II played a significant role. M. W. Graves & Company of Berwick branched out from apples to vegetables in 1940 when contracted by the British Food Ministry to supply 150 tons of dehydrated cabbage and 350 tons of dehydrated potatoes. Dehydration reduced seventy-five pounds of potatoes to nine; when packed into five pound square tins, food had a shelf life of two years. In 1943, Graves expanded operations by opening a new plant in Kentville under the Canada Foods Ltd. name to increase wartime potato production after which pickles became a primary line in the 1950s (right). By 1949, Graves was the largest processor of fruits and vegetables in the Maritimes. Another round of expansion in 1962 resulted in the construction of a Graves frozen food plant at Hillaton (above) where peas, wax and green beans, cauliflower, Brussels sprouts, and vegetable combinations were frozen for markets in Canada, the United States, and Japan.

Processing pickles at Canada Foods Ltd., Kentville, 1950s

CANNING PEARS, SCOTIAN GOLD, 1950s

In the early 1950s, there were several plants in the Valley processing fruits and vegetables. While fresh and frozen produce remain part of the Valley's agricultural based economy today, the last of its vegetable canneries closed out two years ago. Graves, Avon, and Aylmer brands are still very much in evidence on local grocery store shelves but through the tangled maze of mergers and buyouts of the last forty years, all are now processed out-of-province by multinational corporations.

To Scotian Gold goes the honour of being the only member of the recognizable "old guard" that is still Valley owned. When United Fruit Companies of Nova Scotia re-organized in 1957 because of financial woes, the newly structured cooperative assumed the name of Scotian Gold which, as previously mentioned, was purchased in 1945 by United Fruit from the Phinney family. Although processing lines were discontinued more than twenty years ago, Scotian Gold Cooperative Limited, comprised today of fifty-five growers, continues to market a wide variety of locally grown fruits and vegetables. Located on an expansive site at Coldbrook near Kentville, the multi-purpose cooperative provides centralized facilities for storing, packing, and shipping produce, a country store and gardening centre, and a fertilizer plant jointly owned with Co-op Atlantic.

PACKAGING CORN FOR SCOTIAN GOLD, COLDBROOK, 1950s

DON ELLS'S CHICKEN FARM NEAR PORT WILLIAMS, 1950S

Gone are the days of the small family farm when a dozen chickens, a few cows, and a pig or two supplied domestic needs as well as produce to be sold or bartered for groceries and dry goods. In the 1890s, chickens fetched sixty cents a pair and eggs sold for twenty cents a dozen locally or twenty-five to thirty cents in Halifax. The basis for a poultry industry in Nova Scotia began in the late 1800s with the organization of poultry associations and competitive shows. By 1907, seventeen communities in the province were sponsoring annual events, four of which were in the Valley at Windsor, Kentville, Bridgetown, and Bear River. It wasn't until World War II that the nutritional value of eggs came to the fore and the industry grew. The 1940s were also a time when demand increased for broiled chickens in the United States, a market that took another ten or fifteen years to develop in this country. It began with the first "large scale" chicken barbecue ever held in Canada, hosted by the Nova Scotia Agricultural College in Truro on July 1, 1951. The event was such an overwhelming success that it was repeated for three consecutive years with upwards of five thousand people attending on each occasion. Donald F. Archibald of Archibald Farms in Port Williams is credited with building upon this new-found craving in 1956 when he spearheaded the growth of the chicken broiler industry in Nova Scotia. According to agricultural reports, poultry today accounts for one-third of the province's "livestock and products" category for farm cash receipts, fresh eggs being the biggest contributor followed by chicken, then turkey. At least one-half of Nova Scotia's eggs and two-thirds of its chicken and turkey production originates in Kings County, where the poultry industry as a whole employs more people than the Michelin Tire plant in Waterville.

The Windsor and Kingston areas provide nearly one-third of Nova Scotia's feed cattle today. The Armstrong family name has been synonymous with beef farming in Kingston since Walker Armstrong first herded cattle on foot to Windsor (ninety kilometres one way) for rail shipment to Halifax. When trains reached Kingston in 1870, holding pens were built for livestock and Manning Armstrong, Walker's son, travelled the Valley to Digby by horse and cart in search of cattle to buy, in addition to working his own beef and sheep farm. Manning was the first wholesaler to ship meat to Halifax in refrigerated rail cars. In the 1920s, O. H. Armstrong began delivering beef to Halifax twice weekly by truck, a five-hour trip one-way over gravel roads that began at four o'clock in the morning and ended back home at midnight. During the 1930s, the three largest dairy producers in the Valley were W. E. Saunders and Hallet Armstrong, both from Kingston, and Will Currie of Wilmot. The Middleton *Outlook* published a monthly tally of each farm's output for the respective creameries that readers followed like a hockey box score. Creameries were to the dairy farmer what evaporators and canneries were to the apple grower. Kings County had two in 1898—Acadia Dairy Company at Grand Pré and Aylesford Creamery Company. The largest in the province by the 1930s was the Valley Creamery Limited (formerly Cloverdale Creamery) at Kingston. Half a dozen teams made daily pick-up runs between Blomidon and Annapolis Royal, averaging 1,500 kilometres a week and bringing in twelve thousand pounds of cream a month from 2,100 customers. In just one month during 1934 the creamery produced 750,000 pounds of butter. A humorous anecdote involved North Kingston farmer Everett Saunders who, in 1927, was first in the area to switch from hand milking to automation. North Kingston had no electricity and so a gasoline engine was used to power the milking machine, which drew the entire community to Everett's barn for its inaugural run.

In 1918, the Kentville Experimental Station acquired five registered Yorkshire sows and a boar which were the start of a swine herd based at the facility until 1934. Breeders were sold throughout the Maritimes, giving the region a widespread reputation "as a producer of high quality bacon hogs." In 1955, Larsen Wholesalers (now Larsen Meat Packers) opened a beef and pork processing plant at Berwick, which in 1961 became a federally inspected facility. According to 2005 statistics, Nova Scotia has the leanest hogs in Canada, with Kings County producing at least one-half of the province's output. While the current pork market appears healthy, this is not reflected in the region's pork farmers. Studies show provincial hog production has dropped significantly over the last five years and where there were two hundred hog farms in Nova Scotia ten years ago, today there are fewer than one hundred. Many factors have been cited, including a lack of interest by next-generation farmers, cheaper international hog prices, the fluctuating Canadian dollar, and high production costs combined with low returns.

KENTVILLE EXPERIMENTAL STATION DISPLAY, N.D.

The Kentville Experimental Station placed displays such as this one promoting fresh and canned vegetables in the early 1900s at agricultural exhibitions in Halifax, Bridgewater, and Yarmouth.

PARADE FLOAT, 1929

A 1929 parade float publicizes the importance of bee pollination and the benefits of eating honey. One-half of the honey produced today in Nova Scotia comes from the Valley. Traditional farm produce and products still form a large part of the Valley's agricultural economy, but a whole new sector reflective of the changing times has opened up. Addressing the baby boomer generation's consumer demands for a healthier, natural diet, specialty farms and processors now provide a litany of choices that include, in part, licensed free range chickens and eggs, certified organic vegetables and beef, herb vinegars, jellies, mustards, flax flour, granola cereals, hemp seed oils, mushrooms, jelly parfaits, frozen fruit bars, salad kits, cranberry juices, teas, chutney, and stuffing. Valley exports travel the globe to the United States, Latin America, the Caribbean, Iceland, the United Kingdom, and Taiwan.

FARM PRODUCE BOUND FOR MARKET, C.1915

Weekend farmers' markets are popular venues today in many Valley towns where old-time meeting and greeting strengthens the bonds of rural community life.

For at least two hundred years, Valley farmers have been supplying Halifax markets with produce. Historian Arthur Eaton writes, "Before the Windsor & Annapolis Railway was built, all poultry, pork, eggs, butter, etc. were trucked away to Halifax by the farmer himself, who in addition to his own expenses and those of his team was obliged to spend three or four days in marketing a load that now [1910] would not fill one corner of a railway car. Cattle and great flocks of lambs were driven to market, the driver footing it after them, often with blistered feet, and not seldom far into the night, so as to be in Halifax at an early hour the next morning." With completion of the railway to Windsor in the early 1850s, a "piggy back" train service (a first in Canada) was offered for a few years where a farmer paid $1.56 to transport himself, wagon, freight, and horse into Halifax. Valley farmers still come to the city market every week but no longer by train cars; one cooperative even offers an "on-line farmers' market" whereby members can place an order and have produce delivered directly to their door. A 2005 government report on "Farmers' Markets and their Economic Impact in Nova Scotia" concluded that "farmers' markets are local outlets for small producers throughout the province that provide a substantial and widely dispersed impact on the economic well-being of the province." Results showed that customers live within five kilometres of the market and are frequent, long-time patrons. An average expenditure is $28.27 with sales at rural markets lower on average than in Halifax; one-half of respondents spent an additional $34.67 at other businesses because of visiting the markets. The primary reasons given for shopping at farmers' markets are fresh produce, the social atmosphere of the market place, the desire to support local farmers, and high-quality products and organic foods.

A signature trademark of the Valley has long been its roadside fruit and vegetable stands and U-pick farms. A draw for many patrons is the always-popular ice cream and home-baked goods often nearby. Less conspicuous but fun to search out (and a great way to see the countryside) are the occasional end-of-the-lane tables which offer one or two products, a tin can for payment and a refreshing dose of trust for the inherent honesty of man.

YOUNG ENTRE-PRENEURS SELL STRAWBERRIES TO MOTORISTS FROM AN IMPROVISED FRUIT STAND AT KINGSTON, 1950S

Valley people not only grow and sell farm produce, they celebrate its heritage. There are special days galore—harvest festivals, winefests, and ciderfests; pumpkin people, regattas, and frolics; barbeques, breakfasts, suppers, and teas; carnivals, socials, and jamborees. For the last few years, an "Open Farm Day" has been held throughout Atlantic Canada in September with thousands of people visiting more than 140 farms for tours and demonstrations. One-third of the participating Nova Scotian farms traditionally are from the Valley.

HEARTBEAT OF THE VALLEY. "CHEWIN' THE FAT" AT BRIDGETOWN, 1940S

In *Off-Trail In Nova Scotia*, Will R. Bird writes, "No country produces a better crop than its inhabitants and you'll find that Nova Scotians living along the byways in random places have developed a strength of soul to serve in need, a dry humour for conversation, and a philosophy to reinforce cheerfulness that is a precious tonic."

Selected Bibliography

Bruce, Harry. *RA: The Story of RA Jodrey Entrepreneur.* Toronto: McClelland & Stewart, 1979.

Calnek, W. A. *History of the County of Annapolis.* Toronto: William Briggs, 1897.

Comeau, Louis V. *Historic Kentville.* Halifax: Nimbus Publishing, 2003.

Eaton, Arthur Wentworth Hamilton. *The History of Kings County Nova Scotia.* Salem, Mass.: Salem Press, 1910.

Hutten, Anne. *Valley Gold: The Story of the Apple Industry in Nova Scotia.* Halifax: Petheric Press, 1981.

Jones, Elizabeth. *Gentlemen and Jesuits: Quests For Glory And Adventure In The Early Days Of New France.* Toronto: University of Toronto Press, 1986.

Kingston, Greenwood and Vicinity Historical Society. *Echoes Across the Valley: A History of Kingston and Its Neighbours.* 2 volumes. Hantsport: Lancelot Press, 1994.

Lawrence, Ian. *Historic Annapolis Royal.* Halifax: Nimbus Publishing, 2002.

Leonard, Marian (Bishop). *Paradis Terrestre: A History of the Village of Paradise, Nova Scotia.* Paradise Women's Institute: self-published, 1991.

Parker, Mike. *Historic Digby.* Halifax: Nimbus Publishing, 2000.

Pulley, Glen. *A Place in History: Our Time at Macdonald Consolidated School and Macdonald Museum (1903–2003).* Halifax: etc. Press, 2003.

Robertson, Barbara R. *Sawpower, Making Lumber in the Sawmills of Nova Scotia.* Halifax: Nimbus Publishing, 1986.

Sheppard, Tom. *Historic Wolfville, Grand Pré and Countryside.* Halifax: Nimbus Publishing, 2003.

Surette-Draper, Susan. *Return to Acadie, A Self-Guided Memory Walk of the Annapolis Valley.* Societé Promotion Grand-Pré, 2004.

Vaughan, Garth. *Historic Windsor.* Halifax: Nimbus Publishing, 2006.

Wilson, Isaiah W. *A Geography & History of the County of Digby.* Halifax: Holloway Brothers, 1900.

Image Credits

Numbers refer to pages. The letters "t" and "b" stand for top and bottom.
NSARM—Nova Scotia Archives and Records Management
ACHRS—Annapolis County Historical Restoration Society
NSIS—Nova Scotia Information Service

NSARM: 6t, 6b, 7, 10b, 13, 14b, 16t, 16b, 17, 20, 26t, 26b, 30, 31b, 34, 35t, 37t, 37b, 38, 39, 40, 43b, 47b, 48t, 48b, 49t, 49b, 53b, 54, 55t, 55b, 58, 59t, 59b, 60, 61t, 61b, 62, 63, 64, 66, 67b, 68, 69t, 69b, 72, 73, 74, 75, 77t, 77b, 93, 94t, 94b, 95t, 97, 100, 102, 103t, 103b, 104t, 104b, 105t, 105b, 107t, 108, 110, 111t, 111b, 115t, 115b, 116, 117t, 121, 125, 126, 127t, 127b, 128, 129t, 130, 139, 160.
NSARM (ACHRS): 1, 3, 8t, 14t, 29, 32, 33t, 35b, 42, 44, 45b, 46, 47t, 53t, 101t, 101b, 134, 158.
NSARM (NSIS): 4t, 4b, 10t, 12t, 31t, 36, 45t, 65, 83, 87, 90, 91, 92, 96, 98, 109t, 109b, 124, 129b, 141, 145b, 149t, 149b, 150, 151, 152, 153, 154, 156, 159t, 159b.
Blair House Museum: 11, 12b, 15, 113, 114, 122-23, 131, 133b, 135t, 135b, 136, 137b, 138, 144, 145t, 146t, 146b, 147t, 147b, 148, 155.
Kentville Research Station: 132, 133t, 157t, 157b.
Kings County Museum Archives: 33b, 81, 107b, 137t.
Berwick Apple Museum: 120.
Greenwood Military Aviation Museum: 78.

Barb Bishop: 22, 23, 24, 79.
Carole Coleman: 142, 143b.
Barry Corkum: 88t.
Tom Forrestall: 71.
Pat Hampsey: 118-19.
Elke Huber: 106,
Sara Keddy: 140.
Graham McBride: 51.
Gordon Palmer: 19.
Mike Parker: 27b, 56, 57, 99b.
St. Clair Patterson: 27t,
Charles Rawding: 112,
Chris Roop: 143t.
Roger Ryan: 67t, 70.
Murray Saunders: 5, 8b, 41, 43t, 76, 82, 84, 85t, 85b, 89, 117b.
Garry Shutlak: 50.
Trudy Spinney: 80.
Brian Tupper: 9, 25, 52, 86, 99t,
Gordon and Helen Whalyon: 88b.
Dave Whitman: 21.
Kevin Wood: 18t, 18b.